Teaching
Word Recognition, Spelling, and Vocabulary

Strategies From The Reading Teacher

Timothy V. Rasinski

Nancy D. Padak

Brenda Weible Church

Gay Fawcett

Judith Hendershot

Justina M. Henry

Barbara G. Moss

Jacqueline K. Peck

Elizabeth (Betsy) Pryor

Kathleen A. Roskos

Editors

INTERNATIONAL
Reading
Association

800 Barksdale Road, PO Box 8139
Newark, Delaware 19714-8139, USA
www.reading.org

The International Reading Association attempts, through its publications, to provide a forum for a wide spectrum of opinions on reading. This policy permits divergent viewpoints without implying the endorsement of the Association.

Director of Publications   Joan M. Irwin
Editorial Director, Books and Special Projects   Matthew W. Baker
Special Projects Editor   Tori Mello Bachman
Permissions Editor   Janet S. Parrack
Associate Editor   Jeanine K. McGann
Production Editor   Shannon Benner
Editorial Assistant   Pamela McComas
Publications Coordinator   Beth Doughty
Production Department Manager   Iona Sauscermen
Art Director   Boni Nash
Senior Electronic Publishing Specialist   Anette Schütz-Ruff
Electronic Publishing Specialist   Cheryl J. Strum
Electronic Publishing Assistant   John W. Cain

Library of Congress Cataloging-in-Publication Data
Teaching word recognition, spelling, and vocabulary : strategies from The reading teacher / Timothy Rasinski ... [et al.], editors.
    p.   cm.
  Includes bibliographical references.
  ISBN 0-87207-279-7
  1. Word recognition.   2. Reading.   I. Rasinski, Timothy V.   II. Reading teacher.
LB1050.44.T42   2000
372.4—dc21
               00-058192

Contents

About the editors

Timothy V. Rasinski
Professor of Education
Kent State University
Kent, Ohio, USA

Nancy D. Padak
Professor, Education; Director, Reading
    & Writing Center
Kent State University
Kent, Ohio, USA

Brenda Weible Church
Principal of Seiberling Elementary
    School
Akron Public Schools
Akron, Ohio, USA

Gay Fawcett
Executive Director of the Research
    Center for Educational Technology
Kent State University
Kent, Ohio, USA

Judith Hendershot
Teacher
Field Local Schools
Mogadore, Ohio, USA

Justina M. Henry
Literacy Collaborative-Project Trainer
The Ohio State University
Columbus, Ohio, USA

Barbara G. Moss
Research Associate
CASAS
San Diego, California, USA

Jacqueline K. Peck
PT3 Project Director
Kent State University
Kent, Ohio, USA

Elizabeth (Betsy) Pryor
Educational consultant; retired as super-
    visor of K–12 Reading/Language Arts
    for Columbus Public Schools
Worthington, Ohio, USA

Kathleen A. Roskos
Professor
John Carroll University
University Heights, Ohio, USA

Introduction

No effective reading/language arts curriculum would be complete without some attention given to the study of words—how words are decoded, how they are spelled, and what they mean. Research has long demonstrated the connection between word knowledge and overall reading proficiency (Davis, 1944). Indeed, readers' knowledge of words has been shown to be one of the most powerful predictors of reading comprehension (Anderson & Freebody, 1981).

We readily acknowledge that perhaps the best way to improve one's word recognition and increase one's vocabulary is through plenty of authentic contextual reading. Through lots of reading, sight word recognition is improved through the repeated exposure to important words. Moreover, readers see a variety of new words and ideas presented in a meaningful context that will allow them to develop their conceptual knowledge. Thus, the very act of reading itself gives readers many opportunities to learn new words and concepts (Cunningham & Stanovich, 1998). The improvements in word knowledge that occur as a result of real reading lead to improved overall reading performance and, as a result, allow students to "bootstrap" themselves to higher levels of reading performance (Stanovich, 1986).

Effective reading/language arts programs at any level also provide opportunities for students to explore words, how they work, what they mean, and how they are used, in a more focused manner. As teachers draw students' attention to various aspects of words, students are more likely to develop a greater appreciation for words, to use word knowledge in their own reading, and to apply words effectively in their own speech and writing. Whether the focus is spelling, decoding, or word meaning, word study can be a valuable addition to any reading/language arts curriculum.

With *Teaching Word Recognition, Spelling, and Vocabulary*, one of four books in the Teaching Reading Collection, we share with you classroom-tested strategies for helping students learn about words. The articles have been drawn from the Teaching Reading department of *The Reading Teacher* during our 6-year tenure as editors; this section of the journal is devoted to practical reading instruction strategies for classrooms, reading clinics, and homes. The ideas and support materials included in this book are examples of authentic and thoughtful classroom practice. The contributors subscribe to a broad understanding of the importance of literacy learning: That literacy is central to all learning and that literacy is learned through the work of dedicated and caring teachers at every grade level. The purpose of this book, then, is to present teacher-tested ideas, resources, and activities to make word learning and literacy learning more effective and engaging for students.

The articles in this volume were submitted to *The Reading Teacher* by teachers from around the world as examples of best and innovative practice in their classrooms. During our editorship, we received thousands of articles of this type, but only a select few were chosen for publication in the journal. Each article went through a review process that consisted of at least three separate readings and rankings. Only those that were given the highest ratings were published. For this present volume, we examined again those articles that appeared in *The Reading Teacher*. Again we read and rated them, primarily for clarity, purpose, adherence to a particular theme, ease of implementation, and adaptability in a variety of classroom and other educational settings. Only those articles that met these high standards and criteria were chosen for this volume. In this book you are reading the "best of the best" of practical word-study strategies from *The Reading Teacher*.

The ideas and strategies offered in this volume provide possible building blocks for developing word-study routines that are engaging and effective for all students.

We challenge you, as you read this book, to put together the instructional ideas you find most appropriate into a word-study routine that will work for you and your students and meet the objectives of your curriculum.

We have enjoyed our collaboration with the authors of these articles, and we have come to appreciate the tireless work of dedicated and selfless reading teachers around the world. We hope that you, teachers and teacher educators, will find this book helpful, supportive, and energizing as we all work toward a fully literate global society.

TR, NP, JH, BM,
BC, GF, TH,
JP, BP, KR

REFERENCES

Anderson, R.C., & Freebody, P. (1981). Vocabulary knowledge. In J. Guthrie (Ed.), *Comprehension and teaching: Research reviews* (pp. 77–117). Newark, DE: International Reading Association.

Cunningham, A.E., & Stanovich, K.E. (1998). What reading does for the mind. *American Educator, 22*, 8–15.

Davis, F.B. (1944). Fundamental factors of comprehension. *Psychometrika, 9*, 185–197.

Stanovich, K.E. (1986). Matthew effects in reading: Some consequences of individual difference in the acquisition of literacy. *Reading Research Quarterly, 21*, 360–407.

Read-aloud books for developing phonemic awareness: An annotated bibliography

Hallie Kay Yopp

VOLUME 48, NUMBER 6, MARCH 1995

The relationship between phonemic awareness and learning to read is extremely important (Stanovich, 1994). In fact, recent research suggests that phonemic awareness may be the "most important core and causal factor separating normal and disabled readers" (Adams, 1990, p. 305). A critical question, then, is how do children become phonemically aware? Studies reveal that the ability to segment and otherwise manipulate sounds in speech can be explicitly taught to children and that those children who receive training in phonemic awareness perform at higher levels on subsequent reading and spelling achievement tests than their control group counterparts (Ball & Blachman, 1988; Bradley & Bryant, 1983; Cunningham, 1990; Lundberg, Frost, & Peterson, 1988).

Phonemic awareness may also be facilitated in a less direct, but perhaps more natural and spontaneous way, by providing children with language-rich environments in which attention is often turned to language itself by means of word play in stories, songs, and games. Classroom teachers are in the ideal position to capitalize on what Geller's (1982a, 1982b, 1983) observations reveal as children's natural propensity to experiment with sounds in their language. Geller recommends that teachers observe children's play with speech sounds and design activities that stimulate this play, arguing that word play enables children to explore and experiment with systems of sound separate from their meanings and that this has implications for literacy learning. Other researchers have also encouraged teachers to provide their young students with activities that are linguistically stimulating—activities such as word games, rhymes, riddles, and songs (Adams, 1990; Mattingly, 1984; Yopp, 1992).

Probably the most accessible, practical, and useful vehicles to enhance students' sensitivity to the phonological basis of their language are children's books that deal playfully with speech sounds through rhyme, alliteration, assonance, or other phoneme manipulation (Griffith & Olson, 1992). The purpose of this article is to provide teachers with an annotated bibliography of children's literature that draws attention to language sounds and so may be useful in facilitating the acquisition of phonemic awareness.

Criteria for selection

The following three criteria were used for inclusion of books in this bibliography:

1. Play with language is explicit and is a critical, dominant feature of the books so that children are encouraged to shift their focus from the message of the text to the language that is used to communicate the message. Only books that make very obvious use of rhyme, alliteration, assonance, phoneme substitution, or segmentation are included.

2. The books are appropriate for young children. Neither the vocabulary nor the story lines are too advanced for most kindergarten children or first graders. For example, though S. Kellogg's (1987) *Aster Aardvark's Alphabet Adventures* (Morrow Junior Books) makes clever use of alliteration, the vocabulary and content are rather sophisticated: "Entering an elite eating establishment escorted by an enormously eminent elephant...." Thus, the book is inappropriate for this list.

3. The books easily lend themselves to further language play. Their patterns are explicit, their structures readily accessible, and their content simple enough that the stories can be extended.

How to use these books

- Read and reread the story

Read the story aloud several times simply for the pure joy of reading and sharing.

- Comment on the language use

After several readings, teachers may encourage students to comment about the story. Teachers may ask "Did you enjoy the book? Was it fun? What was fun about it?" and let the children discover for themselves that the word play added tremendous entertainment to the story. Or teachers may chuckle at several points in a rereading and say "That was funny! Did you notice how those words rhyme?" or "Did you notice how the character got all mixed up in what he was saying?" and gently guide children's attention to the word play.

- Encourage predictions

Most of these stories are very predictable. Teachers should encourage their students to predict sounds, words, or phrases and then ask the students how they arrived at their predictions. Generally, the answer will address the author's use of language: "He's making the words rhyme!" "She's starting everything with the same sound!"

- Examine language use

Depending upon the children, teachers may wish to examine more closely the language use in a story. Teachers may explicitly point out and analyze phonemic features. With younger children (perhaps ages 3 to 5), simply commenting on the language is likely most appropriate: "Those words start alike! That's silly that the author did that! Listen: kitten, cape, coat." With older children (perhaps ages 4 to 7), closer examinations may be fruitful: "What sound do you hear at the beginning of all those words? Yes—the /k/ sound. Isn't it interesting how the author uses so many words with the /k/ sound? What are some other words that begin with that sound?"

• Create additional verses or make another version of the story

Children can change the story yet maintain the language pattern to develop their own versions of the story. My 3½-year-old son enjoyed listening to *"I Can't," Said the Ant* (Cameron, 1961) and after the first reading began reciting chunks of the story retaining the dialog but changing the speaker. For instance, instead of the author's "'Don't break her!' said the shaker," Peter prefers to say "'Don't break her,' said the baker." He is quite amused by his changes in the story and insists that we read it his way.

After reading *Zoophabets* (Tallon, 1979) each child may wish to make his/her own *Zoophabets* book by drawing pictures of nonsense animals and dictating words to the teacher; or each student could be responsible for a particular letter sound and make a single page of the alphabet book to be included in a class compilation.

After reading *More Bugs in Boxes* (Carter, 1990), children can make their own "open the flap" book with drawings of interesting bugs hidden away under each flap. Each bug represents a particular sound. The child who chooses /s/ may decide to draw six laughing bugs who are looking off to the side and dictate, "six silly bugs looking sideways." Or instead of making a book, children may actually construct boxes, make three dimensional bugs, and have fun naming them: "carrot-eating, colorful cucumber bugs!"

Annotated Bibliography

Brown, M.W. (1993). *Four fur feet*. New York: Doubleday.
  In this simple book, the reader is drawn to the /f/ sound as the phrase "four fur feet" is repeated in every sentence as a furry animal walks around the world. The same pattern is used throughout the story as we see four fur feet walk along the river, into the country, and so forth. The book must be turned around as the animal makes its way around the world.
Buller, J., & Schade, S. (1988). *I love you, good night*. New York: Simon and Schuster.

A mother and child tell each other how much they love one another. When the child says she loves her mother as much as "blueberry pancakes," the mother responds that she loves her child as much as "milkshakes." The child says she loves the mother as much as "frogs love flies," to which the mother responds she loves her child as much as "pigs love pies." The two go back and forth in this manner until

(continued)

"good night" is said. The rhyme invites the listener to participate and continue the story.

Cameron, P. (1961). *"I can't," said the ant*. New York: Coward-McCann.

Household items discuss the fall of a teapot from the counter in a kitchen and the means by which to put it back. In a series of brief contributions to the conversation, each item says something that rhymes with its own name. "'Don't break her,' said the shaker" and "'I can't bear it,' said the carrot."

Carle, E. (1974). *All about Arthur (an absolutely absurd ape)*. New York: Franklin Watts.

Arthur, an accordion playing ape who lives in Atlanta, feels lonely and travels from Baltimore to Yonkers making friends. In each city he makes a friend whose name matches the initial sound of the city, from a banjo-playing bear in Baltimore to a young yak in Yonkers.

Carter, D. (1990). *More bugs in boxes*. New York: Simon and Schuster.

This pop-up book presents a series of questions and answers about make-believe bugs who are found inside a variety of boxes. Both the questions and answers make use of alliteration: "What kind of bug is in the rosy red rectangle box? A bright blue big-mouth bug." Following a similar pattern is the author's *Jingle Bugs* (1992, Simon and Schuster), which has a Christmas theme and makes use of rhyme: "Who's in the chimney, warm and snug? Ho, ho, ho! It's Santa Bug!"

de Regniers, B., Moore, E., White, M., & Carr, J. (1988). *Sing a song of popcorn*. New York: Scholastic.

A number of poems in this book draw attention to rhyme and encourage children to experiment. Also included are poems that play with sounds within words. In "Galoshes" the author describes the slippery slush "as it slooshes and sloshes and splishes and sploshes" around a child's galoshes. In "Eletelephony" sounds are mixed up and substituted for one another: "Once there was an elephant,/Who tried to use the telephant...."

Deming, A.G. (1994). *Who is tapping at my window?* New York: Penguin.

A young girl hears a tapping at her window and asks, "Who is there?" The farm animals each respond, "It's not I," and she discovers that it is the rain. The book is predictable in that each pair of animals rhymes. The loon responds, followed by the raccoon. The dog's response is followed by the frog's.

Ehlert, L. (1989). *Eating the alphabet: Fruits and vegetables from A to Z*. San Diego, CA: Harcourt Brace Jovanovich.

Fruits and vegetables are offered in print and pictures for each letter of the alphabet in this book. The following are displayed for B, for instance: blueberry, brussels sprout, bean, beet, broccoli, banana.

Emberley, B. (1992). *One wide river to cross*. Boston: Little, Brown.

This Caldecott Honor Book is an adaptation of the traditional African American spiritual about Noah's ark. Through the use of rhyme, the author describes the animals gathering on board one by one (while "Japhelth played the big bass drum"), two by two ("The alligator lost his shoe"), and so on up to ten, when the rains begin.

Fortunata. (1968). *Catch a little fox*. New York: Scholastic.

(continued)

A group of children talk about going hunting, identifying animals they will catch and where they will keep each one. A frog will be put in a log, a cat will be put in a hat, and so forth. The story concludes with the animals in turn capturing the children, putting them in a ring and listening to them sing. All are then released. The music is included in this book. A different version of this story that includes a brontosaurus (who is put in a chorus) and armadillo (who is put in a pillow) is J. Langstaff's (1974) *Oh, A-Hunting We Will Go*, published by Atheneum, New York.

Galdone, P. (1968). *Henny Penny*. New York: Scholastic.

A hen becomes alarmed when an acorn hits her on the head. She believes the sky is falling, and on her way to inform the king she meets several animals who join her until they are all eaten by Foxy Loxy. This classic story is included here because of the amusing rhyming names of the animals. A recent release of this story is S. Kellogg's *Chicken Little* (1985), published by Mulberry Books, New York.

Geraghty, P. (1992). *Stop that noise!* New York: Crown.

A mouse is annoyed with the many sounds of the forest and implores the cicada to stop its "zee-zee-zee-zee," the frog to stop its "woopoo," until it hears far more disturbing sounds—the "Brrrm" and "Crrrrrr RACKA-DACKA-RACKA-SHOONG" of a bulldozer felling trees. The presentation of animal and machine sounds makes this book useful in drawing attention to the sounds in our language.

Gordon, J. (1991). *Six sleepy sheep*. New York: Puffin Books.

Six sheep try to fall asleep by slurping celery soup, telling spooky stories, singing songs, sipping simmered milk, and so on. The use of the /s/ sound, prevalent throughout, amuses listeners as they anticipate the sheep's antics.

Hague, K. (1984). *Alphabears*. New York: Henry Holt.

In this beautifully illustrated book, 26 teddy bears introduce the alphabet and make use of alliteration. Teddy bear John loves jam and jelly. Quimbly is a quilted bear, and Pam likes popcorn and pink lemonade.

Hawkins, C., & Hawkins, J. (1986). *Tog the dog*. New York: G.P. Putnam's Sons.

This book tells the story of Tog the dog who likes to jog, gets lost in the fog, falls into a bog, and so forth. With the exception of the final page, where the letters *og* appear in large type, the pages in the book are not full width. As the reader turns the narrower pages throughout the text a new letter appears and lines up with the *og* so that when Tog falls into the bog, for example, a large letter b lines up with *og* to make the word bog. This is a great book for both developing phonemic awareness and pointing out a spelling pattern. Also by the authors are *Jen the Hen* (1985), *Mig the Pig* (1984), and *Pat the Cat* (1993), all published by G.P. Putnam's Sons.

Hymes, L., & Hymes, J. (1964). *Oodles of noodles*. New York: Young Scott Books.

Several of the poems in this collection make use of nonsense words in order to complete a rhyme. In "Oodles of Noodles," the speaker requests oodles of noodles because they are favorite foodles. In "Spinach," the authors list a series of words

(continued)

each beginning with the /sp/ sound until they finally end with the word "spinach." Words include "spin," "span," "spun," and "spoony." Many of the poems point out spelling patterns that will be entertaining with an older audience.

Krauss, R. (1985). *I can fly*. New York: Golden Press.

In this simple book, a child imitates the actions of a variety of animals. "A cow can moo. I can too." "I can squirm like a worm." The rhyming element combined with the charm of the child's imaginative play makes the story engaging. On the final page, nonsense words that rhyme are used, encouraging listeners to experiment with sounds themselves: "Gubble gubble gubble I'm a mubble in a pubble."

Kuskin, K. (1990). *Roar and more*. New York: Harper Trophy.

This book includes many poems and pictures that portray the sounds that animals make. Both the use of rhyme and presentation of animal sounds ("Ssnnaaaarrll" for the tiger, "Hsssssss..." for the snake) draw children's attention to sounds. An earlier edition of this book won the 1979 NCTE Award for Excellence in Poetry for Children.

Lewison, W. (1992). *Buzz said the bee*. New York: Scholastic.

A series of animals sit on top of one another in this story. Before each animal climbs on top of the next, it does something that rhymes with the animal it approaches. For instance, the hen dances a jig before sitting on the pig. The pig takes a bow before sitting on the cow.

Martin, B. (1974). *Sounds of a powwow*. New York: Holt, Rinehart & Winston.

Included in this volume is the song "K-K-K-Katy" in which the first consonant of several words is isolated and repeated, as is the song title.

Marzollo, J. (1989). *The teddy bear book*. New York: Dial.

Poems about teddy bears adapted from songs, jump rope rhymes, ball bouncing chants, cheers, and story poems are presented. Use of rhyme is considerable, from the well known, "Teddy bear, teddy bear, turn around, Teddy bear, teddy bear, touch the ground" to the less familiar, "Did you ever, ever, ever in your teddy bear life see a teddy bear dance with his wife?" and the response, "No I never, never, never...." Play with sounds is obvious in the poem "Teddy Boo and Teddy Bear" where the author says, "Icabocker, icabocker, icabocker, boo! Icabocker, soda cracker, phooey on you!"

Obligado, L, (1983). *Faint frogs feeling feverish and other terrifically tantalizing tongue twisters*. New York: Viking.

For each letter of the alphabet, one or more tongue twisters using alliteration is presented in print and with humorous illustrations. *S* has smiling snakes sipping strawberry sodas, a shy spider spinning, and a swordfish sawing. *T* presents two toucans tying ties, turtles tasting tea, and tigers trying trousers.

Ochs, C.P. (1991). *Moose on the loose*. Minneapolis, MN: Carolrhoda Books.

A moose escapes from the zoo in the town of Zown and at the same time a chartreuse caboose disappears. The zookeeper runs throughout the town asking citizens if they've seen a "moose on the loose in a

(continued)

chartreuse caboose." No one has seen the moose but each has seen a different animal. Included among the many citizens is Ms. Cook who saw a pig wearing a wig, Mr. Wu who saw a weasel paint at an easel, and Mrs. Case who saw a skunk filling a trunk. Each joins in the search.

Otto, C. (1991). *Dinosaur chase*. New York: Harper Trophy.

A mother dinosaur reads her young one a story about dinosaurs in which "dinosaur crawl, dinosaur creep, tiptoe dinosaur, dinosaur seek." Both alliteration and rhyme are present in this simple, colorful book.

Parry, C. (1991). *Zoomerang-a-boomerang: Poems to make your belly laugh*. New York: Puffin Books.

Nearly all of the poems in this collection play with language, particularly through the use of predictable and humorous rhyme patterns. In "Oh my, no more pie," the meat's too red, so the writer has some bread. When the bread is too brown, the writer goes to town, and so forth. In "What they said," each of 12 animals says something that rhymes with its name. For instance, a pup says, "Let's wake up," and a lark says, "It's still dark."

Patz, N. (1983). *Moses supposes his toeses are roses*. San Diego, CA: Harcourt Brace Jovanovich.

Seven rhymes are presented here, each of which plays on language to engage the listener. Rhyme is predictable in "Sweetie Maguire" when she shouts "Fire! Fire!" and Mrs. O'Hair says, "Where? Where?" Alliteration makes "Betty Botter" a tongue twister: "But a bit of better butter—that will make my batter better!" Assonance adds humor to "The tooter" when the tooter tries to tutor two tooters to toot!

Pomerantz, C. (1993). *If I had a paka*. New York: Mulberry.

Eleven languages are represented among the 12 poems included in this volume. The author manipulates words as in "You take the blueberry, I'll take the dewberry. You don't want the blueberry, OK take the bayberry...." Many berries are mentioned, including a novel one, the "chuckleberry." Attention is drawn to phonemes when languages other than English are introduced. The Vietnamese translation of the following draws attention to rhyme and repetition: I like fish, Toy tik ka; I like chicken, Toy tik ga; I like duck, Toy tik veet; I like meat, Toy tik teet.

Prelutsky, J. (1982). *The baby Uggs are hatching*. New York: Mulberry.

Twelve poems describe unusual creatures such as the sneepies, the smasheroo, and the numpy-numpy-numpity. Although some of the vocabulary is advanced (the Quossible has an irascible temper), most of the poems will be enjoyed by young children who will delight in the humorous use of words and sounds. For instance, "The Sneezysnoozer sneezes in a dozen sneezy sizes, it sneezes little breezes and it sneezes big surprises."

Prelutsky, J. (1989). *Poems of A. Nonny Mouse*. New York: Alfred A. Knopf.

A Nonny Mouse finally gets credit for all her works that were previously attributed to "Anonymous" in this humorous selection of poems that is appropriate for all ages. Of particular interest for developing phonemic awareness are poems such as "How much wood would a woodchuck

(continued)

chuck" and "Betty Botter bought some butter."

Provenson, A., & Provenson, M. (1977). *Old Mother Hubbard*. New York: Random House.

In this traditional rhyme, Old Mother Hubbard runs errand after errand for her dog. When she comes back from buying him a wig, she finds him dancing a jig. When she returns from buying him shoes, she finds him reading the news.

Raffi. (1987). *Down by the bay*. New York: Crown.

Two young children try to outdo one another in making up rhymes with questions like, "Did you ever see a goose kissing a moose?" and "Did you ever see a bear combing his hair?" Music is included.

Raffi. (1989). *Tingalayo*. New York: Crown.

Here the reader meets a man who calls for his donkey, Tingalayo, and describes its antics through the use of rhyme and rhythm. Phrases such as "Me donkey dance, me donkey sing, me donkey wearin' a diamond ring" will make children laugh, and they will easily contribute additional verses to this song/story.

Sendak, M. (1990). *Alligators all around: An alphabet*. New York: Harper Trophy.

Using alliteration for each letter of the alphabet, Sendak introduces the reader to the alphabet with the help of alligators who have headaches (for H) and keep kangaroos (for K).

Shaw, N. (1989). *Sheep on a ship*. Boston: Houghton Mifflin.

Sheep sailing on a ship run into trouble when facing a sudden storm. This entertaining story makes use of rhyme (waves lap and sails flap), alliteration (sheep on a ship), and assonance ("It rains and hails and shakes the sails").

Showers, P. (1991). *The listening walk*. New York: Harper Trophy.

A little girl and her father go for a walk with their dog, and the listener is treated to the variety of sounds they hear while walking. These include "thhhhh...", the steady whisper sound of some sprinklers, and "whithh whithh," the sound of other sprinklers that turn around and around. Some phonemes are elongated as in "eeeeeeeyowwwoooo...," the sound of a jet overhead. Some phonemes are substituted as in "bik bok bik bok," the sounds of high heels on the pavement.

Silverstein, S. (1964). *A giraffe and a half*. New York: HarperCollins.

Using cumulative and rhyming patterns, Silverstein builds the story of a giraffe who has a rose on his nose, a bee on his knee, some glue on his shoe, and so on until he undoes the story by reversing the events.

Staines, B. (1989). *All God's critters got a place in the choir*. New York: Penguin.

This lively book make use of rhyme to tell of the places that numerous animals (an ox and a fox, a grizzly bear, a possum and a porcupine, bullfrogs) have in the world's choir. "Some sing low, some sing higher, some sing out loud on the telephone wire."

Seuss, Dr. (1963). *Dr. Seuss's ABC*. New York: Random House.

Each letter of the alphabet is presented along with an amusing sentence in which nearly all of the words begin with the targeted letter. "Many mumbling mice are making midnight music in the moonlight...mighty nice."

(continued)

Seuss, Dr. (1965). *Fox in socks*. New York. Random House.

Before beginning this book, the reader is warned to take the book slowly because the fox will try to get the reader's tongue in trouble. Language play is the obvious focus of this book. Assonance patterns occur throughout, and the listener is exposed to vowel sound changes when beetles battle, ducks like lakes, and ticks and clocks get mixed up with the chicks and tocks.

Seuss, Dr. (1974). *There's a wocket in my pocket*. New York: Random House.

A child talks about the creatures he has found around the house. These include a "nooth grush on my tooth brush" and a "zamp in the lamp." The initial sounds of common household objects are substituted with other sounds to make the nonsense creatures in this wonderful example of play with language.

Tallon, R. (1979). *Zoophabets*. New York: Scholastic.

Letter by letter the author names a fictional animal and, in list form, tells where it lives and what it eats. All, of course, begin with the targeted letter. "Runk" lives in "rain barrels" and eats "raindrops, rusty rainbows, ripped rubbers, raincoats, rhubarb."

Van Allsburg, C. *The Z was zapped*. Boston: Houghton Mifflin.

A series of mishaps befall the letters of the alphabet. A is crushed by an avalanche, B is badly bitten, C is cut to ribbons, and so forth. Other alphabet books using alliteration include G. Base's Animalia (1987), published by Harry N. Abrams, K. Greenaway's (1993) *A Apple Pie*, published by Derrydale, and J. Patience's (1993) *An Amazing Alphabet*, published by Random House.

Winthrop, E. (1986). *Shoes*. New York: Harper Trophy.

This rhyming book surveys familiar and some not-so-familiar types of shoes. The book begins, "There are shoes to buckle, shoes to tie, shoes too low, and shoes too high." Later we discover, "Shoes for fishing, shoes for wishing, rubber shoes for muddy squishing." The rhythm and rhyme invite participation and creative contributions.

Zemach, M. (1976). *Hush, little baby*. New York: E.P. Dutton.

In this lullaby, parents attempt to console a crying baby by promising a number of outrageous things including a mockingbird, a diamond ring, a billy goat, and a cart and bull. The verse is set to rhyme, e.g., "If that cart and bull turn over, Poppa's gonna buy you a dog named Rover," and children can easily innovate on the rhyme and contribute to the list of items being promised.

A final note

The children with whom I have read these books quickly responded to both the form of the language and the content of the text. The books stimulated experimentation with sounds, and children readily, enthusiastically, and often spontaneously innovated on the patterns provided.

Of course, this type of book should not be read to the exclusion of other works of children's literature. Books of this nature should, however, be included in the classroom repertoire of reading experiences, since they can serve as a means to help young children attend to and play with the phonemes in their language.

REFERENCES

Adams, M.J. (1990). *Beginning to read: Thinking and learning about print*. Cambridge, MA: MIT Press.

Ball, E., & Blachman, B. (1988). Phoneme segmentation training: Effect on reading readiness. *Annals of Dyslexia, 38,* 208–225.

Bradley, L., & Bryant, P. (1983). Categorizing sounds and learning to read—A causal connection. *Nature, 301,* 419–421.

Cunningham, A.E. (1990). Explicit versus implicit instruction in phonemic awareness. *Journal of Experimental Child Psychology, 50,* 429–444.

Geller, L.G. (1982a). Grasp of meaning in children: Theory into practice. *Language Arts, 59,* 571–579.

Geller, L.G. (1982b). Linguistic consciousness-raising: Child's play. *Language Arts, 59,* 120–125.

Geller, L.G. (1983). Children's rhymes and literacy learning: Making connections. *Language Arts, 60,* 184–193.

Griffith, P.L., & Olson, M.W. (1992). Phonemic awareness helps beginning readers break the code. *The Reading Teacher, 45,* 516–523.

Lundberg, I., Frost, J., & Peterson, O. (1988). Effects of an extensive program for stimulating phonological awareness in preschool children. *Reading Research Quarterly, 23,* 263–284.

Mattingly, I. (1984). Reading, linguistic awareness, and language acquisition. In J. Downing & R. Valtin (Eds.), *Language awareness and learning to read* (pp. 9–25). New York: Springer-Verlag.

Stanovich, K.E. (1994). Romance and reality. *The Reading Teacher, 47,* 280–291.

Yopp, H.K. (1992). Developing phonemic awareness in young children. *The Reading Teacher, 45,* 696–703.

The Bag Game: An activity to heighten phonemic awareness

Nancy K. Lewkowicz

VOLUME 47, NUMBER 6, MARCH 1994

To succeed at beginning reading, children must be aware of the individual phonemes (sounds) within spoken words. Fortunately, phonemic awareness is not simply a function of genetics or maturation; rather, it can be developed and strengthened through instruction and practice (Adams, 1990). But keeping children interested and involved during literacy instruction is also critical to success, as whole language advocates point out. The challenge, then, is how to reconcile these two necessary—but not necessarily compatible—tasks: keeping children actively engaged and providing sufficient focus on the sound within words. How can the kind of enthusiasm generated by reading appealing and high quality literature be maintained in supplementary activities requiring attention to phonemes—those elusive elements rarely brought to consciousness during everyday use of language? One activity that meets this challenge is writing: having children write their own original stories, deriving the needed spellings partly by listening to the sounds of the words. But there are additional means available for arousing and sustaining interest in speech sounds. In particular, games can be designed that hold children spellbound while focusing attention squarely on the phonemic structure of words. And such games can be started at the very earliest stages of literacy instruction, well before children can be expected to deduce spellings or read connected text. The Bag Game keeps a whole group of kindergartners or first graders absorbed and entertained while heightening their awareness of initial consonant phonemes in spoken words. In each round of the game, one child detects and produces the initial consonant sound of a spoken word, and a second child, on hearing that consonant sound, matches it to the original word. But all the children, even those who are currently onlookers, are gripped by the drama of the game and involve themselves in silently articulating and predicting the correct response. This is a game that children request over and over.

Equipment needed

Two large bags, boxes, or totes that can stand alone. The containers must not be transparent. Colorful and attractive ones are best.

Several pairs of familiar objects small enough so that four at a time can fit in one of the bags, but large enough to be seen clearly by the entire group. The names of these objects should begin with consonant sounds to which the children have recently been introduced. Examples: *mit*tens, *sh*oes, (bar of) *s*oap, *f*eathers, *p*encils, (toy) *t*urtles. The members of each pair need not be identical; they can have different colors or patterns—e.g., two unmatched mittens.

Procedures

1. Have the group name the four kinds of objects, as one member of each pair is put into each bag.

2. Select one child to be the Sounder and another to be the Matcher. (In demonstrating the game for the first time, the teacher should take the role of the Sounder.)

3. The Sounder and the Matcher each receive one of the bags, which can be placed on neighboring chairs or low tables. They should not be able to see into each other's bags.

4. The Sounder looks into his or her bag, reaches in, and grasps one of the four objects, keeping it hidden from view. He or she utters just the initial consonant sound of the object, loud and clear.

5. The Matcher, having heard this initial sound, grasps the object in his or her own bag that begins with the sound and lifts it into full view.

6. The Sounder then raises into view the object he or she was holding, for the dramatic test: Do the initial consonant sounds of the two objects match? (If they do—and they almost always do—the group is likely to cheer spontaneously.)

7. Choose two other children and repeat steps 2 through 7. At some point, or on other occasions, substitute different pairs of objects.

Note: Before playing this game, the children should have some experience focusing on initial consonant sounds (with or without the associated printed letters). Stretching (prolonging) the initial sound is useful, for consonants that permit it: "fffffffeather." Initial sounds that cannot be stretched (*p*, *t*, etc.) can be repeated: "p-p-p-pencil." (It is important that the children perform these preliminary vocal activities themselves, rather than just hearing the teacher perform them. This will familiarize them with the oral feel of the sounds, which can then serve as a valuable auxiliary clue in recognizing the sound within a word and in mastering sound-letter correspondences.) In the unlikely event that either the Sounder or the Matcher does not correctly associated object and initial sound, the teacher should carefully lead the child through one of these familiar preliminary activities to help the child made the correct association. Recognition of the importance of phonemic awareness has been described as "the single most powerful advance in the science and pedagogy of reading this century" (Adams, 1991, p. 392). The evidence is in that "games and activities designed to enhance phonemic awareness are shown to accelerate reading and spelling acquisition among beginners and to result in significant recovery among children with reading difficulties" (Adams, 1991, p. 393). The challenge for teachers is to win over the children by making phonemic awareness training interesting. Activities like the Bag Game, in which children find enjoyment in recognizing sounds in their natural setting within meaningful words, can make an important contribution.

REFERENCES

Adams, M.J. (1990). *Beginning to read*. Cambridge, MA: MIT Press.
Adams, M.J. (1991). Response portions of *Beginning to read*: A critique by literacy professionals and a response. *The Reading Teacher, 44,* 370–395.

The use of word analogy instruction with developing readers

Kelly Ann HuffBenkoski
Scott C. Greenwood

VOLUME 48, NUMBER 5, FEBRUARY 1995

A nalogies are powerful tools for teaching creative and critical thinking. There are great rewards to be had in all the subject areas when analogies are used with young readers to create thought patterns. Historically, analogic reasoning has been measured in various types of standardized tests, but recently there has been increased interest in analogy instruction to aid in reading comprehension, vocabulary development, and connection of ideas across the curriculum (Greenwood, 1988; Judy, Alexander, Kulikowich, & Wilson, 1988; Silkebakken & Camp, 1993). Although these writers generally looked at older children, we have developed a procedure for second graders that we share here.

The class chronicled here consists of 24 heterogeneously grouped 7 and 8 year olds, including several with identified special needs. Instructional time and materials are organized entirely around cross-curricular thematic units (e.g., Native Americans, rain forest, ocean, underground, environment, nutrition). Most of the words for the analogies given here are taken from these units. The process we highlight here convinced us that, with appropriate instruction and guidance, younger readers can also find success with word analogies.

Introducing analogies

We begin introducing analogies to second graders by drawing a pair of mittens and a pair of boots on the chalkboard. We ask, "How are mittens and boots the same?" (Both help keeps parts of the body warm and dry.) Then we ask, "On what parts of your body do you wear mittens? On what part of your body do you wear boots?" We then write the following analogy on the chalkboard: *Mittens* are to *hands* as *boots* are to *feet*. We then tell the students that the sentence on the chalkboard is an analogy.

Next, we introduce several more entire analogies (e.g., *pork* is to *pig* as _____ is to *cow*; *cold* is to *ice* as *hot* is to _____) with one-word answers. Then we reverse the order of the same simple pairs in order to stress the importance of sequence in analogies.

Because modeling is so important in learning, it is crucial that we demonstrate our own reasoning processes through the use of think-aloud strategies. We then ask the students to express their reasoning for the answers they give. After some discussion, the group arrives at a definition. The children typically state something to the effect that "an analogy shows in what way different things are alike."

Grouping activities

Next students are presented with four words and are asked to select the word that does not belong. At this stage we include at least some vocabulary that had been introduced previously in their thematic unit instruction.

Some examples are:

(1) kitten bear   puppy   colt

(2) shark   whale   tuna   barracuda

(3) teepee hogan   apartment longhouse

(4) fins   scales paws   gills

Discussion follows as to how the words are classified and which word does not belong. Divergent answers are encouraged as long as they can be supported with logical reasoning. The students are then given groups of three words and are asked to supply a word of their own that does belong with the grouping. Some examples are:

fall, spring, summer, _____

egg, adult, pupa, _____

blue, yellow, green, _____

We encourage the students to verbalize their reasoning processes. We feel that it is important for the students to see that shades of meaning are important and that there can be more than one correct answer. We try to guide the children's recognition that there may be better or more precise answers, depending on the reasoning offered by the student.

For example, we might present the following group of three words and ask the students to supply a word of their own that belongs with the grouping: mittens, sweater, coat, _____. One child might reason that the three items are all things you wear and will complete the group with the word *shorts*. We do not consider this to be an incorrect answer, but we use it as an opportunity to sample the group for other responses and also to think aloud ourselves, looking for a more precise answer. Eventually the students will come up with a fourth item of the group that is indicative of the fact that the original set consists of winter clothing.

The final part of the grouping stage, after deleting and adding, involves stating precisely the relationship between a pair of words. Sometimes called *stem sentences* or *bridge sentences*, these are critical tools to lead the children back to whole analogies. For instance, we might start the students with the words *toucan* and *feathers* and ask them to make a sentence that clearly states the relationship between the two words, keeping them in sequence. We are looking for a sentence such as "A *toucan* is covered with *feathers*." Some examples are:

> <u>see</u> is to <u>eyes</u>
> You see with your eyes.
> <u>octopus</u> is to <u>eight</u>
> An octopus has eight legs.

Whole analogies

Now three-part analogies are written on the board, such as:

> <u>mitten</u> is to <u>hand</u> as <u>sock</u> is to _____
> <u>Thumper</u> is to <u>rabbit</u> as _____ is to <u>deer</u>

Students are encouraged again to expand their conceptual thinking by listening to peers explain their thoughts. One of the most important means of helping students reflect on their own thinking is to have them listen to and appreciate alternative perspectives.

Next, students receive a teacher-made handout. Several are done together with follow-up discussion. Students complete the rest on their own, and a class discussion follows. Some examples are:

> <u>prairie dog</u> is to <u>desert</u> as _____ is to <u>rain forest</u>
> <u>ant</u> is to <u>insect</u> as <u>spider</u> is to _____
> _____ is to <u>dragonfly</u> as <u>caterpillar</u> is to <u>butterfly</u>
> <u>stalactite</u> is to top as _____ is to <u>bottom</u>

At this juncture, several key points need to be reinforced. The examples of rich vocabulary we use with students have been previously introduced and repeatedly used in their thematic unit instruction. Also, the procedure is utilized over many sessions throughout the year.

The next stage is one of the children's favorites, for it is informal and gamelike. The children love to come up with analogies in an effort to stump not only their classmates but also their teachers.

Using a piece of butcher paper, and working in cooperative groups, the students brainstorm their own analogies. One child gives three parts of the analogy, and other children complete it. Here are some examples that our second-grade students have produced during group activities, with the answer in italics:

> <u>bee</u> is to *<u>insect</u>* as <u>toucan</u> is to <u>bird</u>
> <u>heater</u> is to <u>warm</u> as *<u>air conditioner</u>* is to <u>cold</u>
> <u>desert</u> is to <u>dry</u> as <u>rain forest</u> is to *<u>wet</u>*
> <u>book</u> is to *<u>read</u>* as <u>television</u> is to <u>watch</u>
> <u>Algonquin</u> is to <u>wigwam</u> as <u>Iroquois</u> is to *<u>longhouse</u>*
> *<u>cold blooded</u>* is to <u>fish</u> as <u>warm blooded</u> is to <u>mammal</u>
> <u>starfish</u> is to <u>five</u> as <u>blue crab</u> is to *<u>ten</u>*
> <u>car</u> is to <u>gas</u> as <u>sailboat</u> is to *<u>wind</u>*

As was stressed earlier, more than one correct answer is often possible. We need to help students reach beyond limits of their own experiences and enter the experiences of others. The social aspects of the learning involved in this stage are exciting. Working in groups requires the children to justify their ideas and to test the feasibility of their solutions. The children must listen and seek consensus. Completing analogies as a group builds a sense of community. The opportunity to contribute not only improves the quality of students' thinking but builds self-esteem and a sense of connection with the world around them. It demonstrates that their thinking is valued and that what they think can make a difference.

The final stage involves having the students individually create analogies that they share. Divergent answers are encouraged as long as the students can supply cogent explanations for their reasoning. Some examples of student-generated analogies are:

fish is to <u>aquarium</u> as <u>bird</u> is to <u>cage</u>

<u>6</u> is to <u>12</u> as <u>8</u> is to _16_

<u>Danielle</u> is to <u>7</u> as <u>Bronson</u> is to <u>8</u>

<u>disc</u> is to <u>computer</u> as _tape_ is to <u>VCR</u>

<u>hill</u> is to _little_ as <u>mountain</u> is to <u>big</u>

<u>yellowjacket</u> is to <u>sting</u> as <u>giant water-bug</u> is to _bite_

Analogy observations

Our second graders did their best when the analogies in the earlier stages of instruction were teacher made and reflected what they had recently learned. We made analogies from geometry symbols and abstract symbols as well as words and ideas.

We noted that when choices were given to complete an analogy, the children had more trouble picking the "right" choice than when they completed the analogy with no choice answers. This seemed to be especially true when answers all reflected information about the object. For example, _lock_ is to _key_ as _violin_ is to_____ [instrument, bow, music]. Sentence or whole analogies were easier than "add one more item to the group."

Younger children required relevant material tied to a thematic unit or topic. Older children were more worldly in their background knowledge and thus had more success with a mixture of topics.

Excellent discussions about word meanings and the relationship of words to each other came out of analogy instruction. The lessons stressed attention to detail and accurate reading. Our students enjoyed playing with words and were highly motivated and excited when working with analogies.

REFERENCES

Greenwood, S.C. (1988). How to use analogy instruction to reinforce vocabulary. *Middle School Journal, 19*(2), 11–13.

Judy, J.E., Alexander, P.A., Kulikowich, J.M., & Wilson, Y.L. (1988). Effects of two instructional approaches and peer tutoring on gifted and non-gifted sixth-grade students' analogy performance. *Reading Research Quarterly, 23*, 236–255.

Silkebakken, G.P., & Camp, D.J. (1993). A five-step strategy for teaching analogous reasoning to middle school students. *Middle School Journal, 24*(4), 47–50.

The letterbox lesson: A hands-on approach for teaching decoding

Bruce A. Murray
Theresa Lesniak

VOLUME 52, NUMBER 6, MARCH 1999

Mary Claire Whipple, a preservice teacher at Auburn University in Alabama, USA, writes of her experience tutoring a first grader struggling to learn to read:

> In the very beginning of tutoring, we began reading preprimer books. When Susan would come across an unfamiliar word, she would look at the beginning letters and guess the word (which was almost always incorrect). She rarely paid attention to the whole word. In her writing, Susan would sometimes leave out vowels and would only write the consonant sounds.
>
> By the end, I noticed that Susan would stop at an unfamiliar word and would look at each letter. If she felt it was necessary, she would use her finger to cover up parts of the word to help her decode it. She would generate a sound for each letter (or for each familiar letter blend), and then generate a pronunciation of the whole word.
>
> I feel that through the letterbox lessons Susan has learned to pay attention to all parts of the word, not just the first

sound. I have also noticed that she now includes all sounds in her writing of words. (M.C. Whipple, personal communication, May 30, 1997)

Letterbox lessons are hands-on activities for learning the alphabetic code. Children spell words by placing letters in boxes that show the number of phonemes in words, and later they read the words they have spelled. Letterbox lessons lead emergent readers to understand the alphabetic writing system and help beginning readers develop sight vocabulary. Children enjoy letterbox lessons because they experience success and discover that spellings are meaningful ways to represent words.

Why letterbox lessons?

Do you know children who aren't learning to read? Perhaps they come from homes where literacy is not the first priority. You've tried all the activities that work with most children, but they can't remember the words you teach them. They can recite predictable books by looking at pictures or beginning letters and guessing, but they can't read independently.

Many beginners don't realize that English words are written in an ingenious alphabetic code. This code works at a very subtle level, representing with letters the sequence of phonemes our mouths traverse as we say a word. The problem is, phonemes are very hard to detect. They fly by in normal speech at 10–20 phonemes per second, and they overlap with other phonemes in words (Liberman & Liberman, 1992). When children can't see the connection between letters and phonemes, printed words seem like arbitrary strings of symbols, and consequently, they are very difficult to remember.

Letterbox lessons help children work out the spellings of words before trying to read them. Children pay closer attention to the phonemes that letters represent in spelling than in reading (Adams, 1990; Bryant & Bradley, 1985). By spelling words first, they transfer this careful spelling analysis over into reading. In the letterbox lesson, children spell a carefully selected group of words using manipulatives, and then they read the same words.

Children make the most rapid progress when decoding work is explicit and systematic (Spiegel, 1992). Here explicit means the teacher models how to spell and how to sound out and blend to identify words. Systematic means the teacher works through important correspondences in a planned sequence. Explicit, systematic instruction is particularly important for children without extensive preschool literacy preparation (Delpit, 1988). Letterbox lessons teach a systematic sequence of correspondences by the use of explicit instruction.

Decoding instruction will make little difference unless students apply what they learn in reading and writing whole texts. At Auburn University, we have placed letterbox lessons into a tutoring framework modeled after Reading Recovery, a program that emphasizes functional and motivating work with whole texts (Iversen & Tunmer, 1993; Pinnell, Fried, & Estice, 1990). We have obtained our best results when letterbox lessons merge into authentic reading and writing activities, particularly with books that are decodable according to children's current correspondence knowledge. In the discussion that follows, we explain how to use the letterbox lesson for individual hands-on decoding instruction.

Teaching letterbox lessons

To conduct a letterbox lesson, you (a) introduce and model a useful correspondence, (b) provide a carefully selected sequence of words for the student to spell using letterboxes as scaffolds, and then (c) help the student read these same words.

Materials. Letterbox lessons require letter manipulatives and Elkonin boxes (letterboxes). Letter manipulatives are commercially manufactured from many materials, and they can be made from paper or card stock. We use a laser printer and photocopier to print double-sided letters, with capital letters on one side and lowercase letters on the other (see Figure 1). The double-sided sheets are laminated before the letters are cut apart and stored in plastic pages designed for holding photographic slides. Letterbox lessons require both capital and lowercase letters, with extra copies of lowercase vowels and common consonants.

Elkonin boxes are named for Russian psychologist D.B. Elkonin, a pioneer in phoneme awareness research. The visual boxes or squares show the student the number of distinct vocal gestures or phonemes (not letters) in the words to be spelled. For example, the word *sheet* contains only three phonemes. Elkonin boxes are common tools in Reading Recovery lessons (Pinnell et al., 1990). Reading Recovery teachers draw Elkonin boxes on a student's paper to scaffold invented spellings. Knowing how many phonemes to spell helps the student devise more complete invented spellings, enhancing phoneme awareness. Letterboxes are Elkonin boxes made of card stock squares. The squares are taped into rows for placement of letter manipulatives (see Figure 2).

The teacher introduces digraphs (e.g., *th*, *ee*) by taping together single laminated letters. Since digraph spellings require two or three letters, letterboxes must be considerably larger than the letter manipulatives.

Deciding which correspondence to teach. Letterbox lessons are built around a single new correspondence, usually a vowel that a student has not yet learned. Only one correspondence is taught per lesson to avoid overwhelming the student. Identifying the correspondences that the student needs and is ready to learn takes a sharp eye. The best way to decide which correspondence to teach next is by studying a student's miscues during oral reading. For example, if the reader has misread several words with short-*e* vowels, we can infer that the single vowel *e* is not cuing the phoneme /e/; a lesson about the short-*e* vowel is warranted. Another student may not yet recognize that *t* paired with *h* represents a unique phoneme /th/ rather than a succession of consonants, justifying a lesson with words like *thin*, *bath*, and *with*.

Short vowels work well for early letterbox lessons. Though their phonemes

Figure 1
Making letter manipulatives for a letterbox lesson

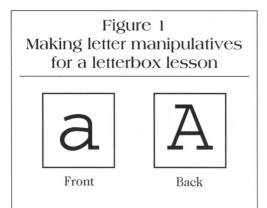

Front   Back

Letter manipulatives are approximately 1 by 1.5 inches (2.5 by 4 cm). Inexpensive manipulatives can be made of paper so that capitals appear on one side and lowercase letters on the other. They are printed so that the printed sheets of capital and lowercase letters can be matched back to back. The matched sheets are then photocopied double-sided, laminated, and cut to size.

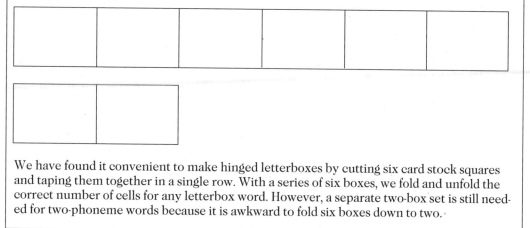

Figure 2
Making letterboxes

Letterboxes (Elkonin boxes) are easily made by cutting 4-inch (10 cm) squares from colored card stock, outlining each square with a marker, and then taping together a horizontal series of squares.

We have found it convenient to make hinged letterboxes by cutting six card stock squares and taping them together in a single row. With a series of six boxes, we fold and unfold the correct number of cells for any letterbox word. However, a separate two-box set is still needed for two-phoneme words because it is awkward to fold six boxes down to two.

are hard to identify, short vowels can be spelled with one letter, and they are common in early instructional texts. If the student doesn't know any short vowel phonemes, short *i* or *a* might be good for starters. Teaching any new correspondence effectively, especially an elusive short vowel, requires that you teach the identity of the phoneme. To teach the phoneme, model its pronunciation and show how the phoneme is part of several example words. It is often helpful to teach the child an alliteration that emphasizes the new phoneme ("Uncle was upset because he was unable to put his umbrella up," Wallach & Wallach, 1976). Then explain that *u* stands for the sound /u/ that we hear in *uncle, upset, unable, umbrella,* and *up*, stretching and exaggerating

the phoneme in the example words. If possible, connect the phoneme with children's experiences. For instance, we often say /u/ ("uh") when we can't remember something. Useful texts for teaching phonemes include alphabet books (Murray, Stahl, & Ivey, 1996), songs (Yopp, 1992), and children's books featuring phonemes (Opitz, 1998).

We have found that teaching vowel correspondences is particularly productive because the correspondences equip students with the decoding knowledge to tackle longer words. After short vowels are mastered, later letterbox lessons can progress through long vowels signaled by silent *e* and vowel digraphs. Lessons on consonant digraphs (e.g., *sh, th, ch*) provide variety and illustrate some of the complexities of the English alphabet.

Selecting words. The heart of a successful letterbox lesson is a carefully selected list of words that illustrate a new correspondence. The best example words are simple, regularly spelled words that feature the correspondence you are teaching. Lists of word families or phonograms (e.g., Fry, 1998) make the task of selecting words much easier. For example, imagine your student needs to learn the short vowel *a* and can use most single consonants. You might select the words *ad, am, an, sad, Sam, man, sand,* and *damp.* Consonant clusters (*nd, mp*) introduce special difficulties in identifying phonemes and should be used sparingly in early lessons, but as children acquire facility with words, they enjoy conquering these word challenges.

Plan a sequence of regular one-syllable words, progressing from simple two- and three-phoneme words to longer words with consonant clusters, excluding words with any unfamiliar correspondences. In choosing words, do not confine your sequence to a single phonogram pattern. Our practice has led us to believe that limiting lessons to words within a single word family is suboptimal because children tend to focus on initial consonants and gloss over the rest of the spelling. For instance, if you give *bat, cat, fat, hat, mat, pat, rat,* and *sat,* the student can simply use initial consonant cues without looking further into the spelling. If you have introduced the short *a* vowel, use a mix of spelling patterns (e.g., *cab, mad, rag, pal, fan,* and *rap*) so that the student is required to look beyond the initial letter. Also, include four- and five-

Word lists for teaching various correspondences				
Short *a*	Short *e*	Short *i*	Short *o*	Short *u*
at, cab, fad, rag, ham, hand, last, stand	Ed, hen, red, pet, end, best, send, spent	it, lid, him, pin, rip, slim, fist, print	Oz, rob, nod, hop, pot, stop, frog, blond	up, rub, bug, sun, gum, stub, bust
Long *a* (a-e)	Long *e* (ee, ea)	Long *i* (i-e)	Long *o* (o-e)	Long *u* (u-e)
fad, fade, Sam, same, snake, trade, flame, planes	eel, fed, feed, stem, steam, sleep, speak, street	Ike, rid, ride, bit, bite, drive, slime, stride	cone, hop, hope, not, note, smoke, stone, stroke	use, dud, dude, June, crude, flute, prune
ch	*sh*	*th*	*ck*	*ng*
chin, chop, chat, chest, chip, chug, much, such, rich, inch, lunch	ash, ship, shot, shop, shut, wish, fish, rush, dish, crash, flash, fresh	with, path, bath, thing, thick, cloth, fifth, think, thank	back, rock, sick, lock, kick, check, chick, thick, stick, black, truck	sing, long, bang, lung, ring, song, thing, bring, swing, spring, strong

phoneme words with consonant clusters (e.g., *last, stand*).

Select a reasonable number of words, usually 5 to 10, scaling the number and complexity of words to the student's ability. It is better to plan for a couple of extra words (which you can omit if the student is struggling) than to have too few. However, it is important to limit the word set so that the student can experience success and move on to other activities. The Table gives examples of word lists to teach various correspondences.

While children need to learn some common irregular words to read nearly any text (e.g., *of, you, have, was, to*), the letterbox lesson is not designed for these exception words. Words for the letterbox lesson illustrate the alphabetic principle by using simple one-to-one matches between letters or digraphs and phonemes. Irregular words with exceptional correspondences provide confusing nonexamples of these matches (for example, *what* does not illustrate the usual pronunciation of the vowel *a*). Also, the lesson is designed for learning one-syllable words. Polysyllabic words are difficult to break down into phonemes because the syllable segmentation confuses the phoneme segmentation.

The words you select for the letterbox lesson need not come from the storybooks your student is reading, nor from miscue records. Students' miscues reveal correspondences and spelling patterns to be learned, but a miscue word rarely makes a good example word; for example, it may be polysyllabic, use untaught correspondences, or have an irregular spelling. Complex and irregular words will be learned as your student acquires better decoding tools. Knowledge of the spelling system will help students teach themselves the tens of thousands of words they will need to learn.

Beginning the lesson. Begin a letterbox lesson by explaining to the student what you hope to accomplish in the lessons. You might say, "Our letterbox lessons will help us see that spellings are really maps of the sounds in words. As you learn the secrets of how words are written, you'll find that spellings really do make sense, and words will become a lot easier to read and remember."

Then explain and model the particular correspondence you are teaching. For example, to teach the *o-e* pattern, you might say, "Today we are working with *o* when the word ends with *e*. The *e* on the end of the word is silent, and it usually means for the *o* to say its name, /O/. For example, here's the word *hop* with *o* all by itself" (spell *hop* in three letterboxes). "If I add a silent *e*, I'm sending a signal to say /O/, its name, instead of /o/" (add an *e* after the third letterbox). "Now I've written *hope*. If I see an *o*-word that ends in *e*, that usually means it has the /O/ sound, and the *e* is silent. For example, I might run into this word" (spell *home* without the letterboxes). "I'm going to think of the /O/ sound as I read this word: /hO · m/, *home*."

Spelling the words. Give the student only the letter manipulatives to spell the words in your lesson. To save time, collect these letters before the lesson, and put away all your other letters. If you are using double-sided letters, ask the student to turn all the letters to the lowercase side. Place the letterbox set that matches the first word to be spelled before the student. Use the letterbox set with the same number of cells as the number of phonemes in the word, not necessarily the number of letters. For example, the correct box for the word *hope* has three cells because the spoken word *hope* has three phonemes, /h/O/p/.

Ask the student to spell the first word (say, *am*) by placing the letter manipulatives in the two-cell letterbox. If the student is successful in spelling a word, rec-ognize that success and move on to the next word. Do not ask a student to sound out and blend a word he or she just spelled; your student will simply repeat it rather than working out its pronunciation. However, if you ask the student to read it later in the lesson, he or she will apply new information to decode the word.

A special adaptation is necessary to introduce silent *e* patterns in letterbox lessons, e.g., that the vowel *i* followed by a consonant and silent *e* usually signals /I/ (long *i*). In such lessons, the silent *e* is placed after the final letterbox. Silent *e*

Summary of the letterbox lesson

1. Design your lesson around a single new correspondence the child needs and is ready to learn. This is usually a vowel spelling.
2. Create a set of 3–12 simple, regular, one-syllable words that illustrate this correspondence. Omit words that involve irregular spellings or any correspondences your student doesn't know. For the easiest letterbox lesson, begin with two-phoneme words that start with vowel (e.g., *up*). Use words with three, four, five, or even six phonemes as your student gains decoding power.
3. Place all letters to be used in the lesson in front of the student. Put aside all other letters.
4. Explain the new correspondence. Make sure the student can identify its phoneme and understands its spelling. Model how to spell and read a couple of example words.
5. Have the student spell each word in the appropriate letterbox set. The letterbox set shows the student how many phonemes to look for in the spoken word and to represent in the spelling. Digraphs (e.g., *th*, *ea*) are placed in a single box, and silent *e*'s are placed after the final box.
6. As each word is spelled, compliment the student and move on at a businesslike pace. Do not ask the student to read the word just spelled.
7. If the student misspells a word, pronounce what was written and ask for a correction. If the student can't make the correction, model the spelling and come back to that word after the other words are spelled.
8. After all the words have been spelled, put away the letterboxes, spell the same words for the student, and ask the student to read each word.
9. If the student is unable to read a word, try uncovering part of the word at a time, or help the student blend the vowel first. If the student is unable to resolve the word after brief help, model the decoding and come back to that word after the other words are read.

Note: A letterbox lesson requires approximately 10 minutes to complete.

does not occupy a box because it does not represent a phoneme in the word; rather, it signals the vowel to "say its name." Word lists for silent *e* lessons should include a mix of short- and long-vowel words so that the student can understand the function of silent *e* as a long-vowel signal.

Letterbox lessons often introduce correspondences that require more than one letter, including consonant digraphs (*ch, sh, th, ck, ng, tch, dge,* etc.), vowel digraphs (*ai, ay, ee, ea, igh, oa, ow, ew, oo,* etc.), vowel diphthongs (*oi, oy, ou, ow, au, aw,* etc.), and *r*-controlled vowels (*ar, er, ir, or, ur,* etc.). The student should bunch the letters representing each phoneme into a single letterbox. Again, it may be helpful at first to tape multiletter correspondences together to help the student remember that they represent a single phoneme. After the student has used the digraph correspondence a few times, remove the tape so that the student selects and groups the letters independently.

Dealing with misspelled words. If a student spells a word incorrectly, usually the most helpful response is to (a) pronounce the misspelled word exactly as it is written and (b) ask the student to fix the spelling. If necessary, (c) model and explain the correct spelling, and (d) come back to that word a few minutes later.

Sometimes a student simply needs time for self-correction. For instance, when Shantae spelled *stuck* as "sutck," she corrected herself after studying what she had written. At other times, it helps to model the spelling for the student by pronouncing what the student has devised ("You spelled *bets*. I'll show you how to spell *best*.") and modeling how to spell the original word, thinking aloud about the phonemes in the word and the order they are heard. In contrast, asking the student questions ("What sound comes first?") is often confusing and counterproductive.

Invented spellings that preserve the order of phonemes are correct for the purposes of a letterbox lesson. For example, if a student spells the word *bell* as "bel," each phoneme has been represented. The teacher can add a second *l* as she compliments the successful spelling, telling the student that the double-*l* spelling is one people have agreed on. When one of our first graders devised the spelling "banc," her tutor complimented the invention and gracefully edited it to *bank*.

Reading the words. In part two of the letterbox lesson, the student reads the words he or she has spelled without the letterboxes. Letterboxes are scaffolds for spelling words; they do not help the student read words. Tell the student, "You spelled all the words. Now it's my turn to work. You tell me what I'm spelling." Then the teacher uses the letter manipulatives to spell each of the words for the student read.

Using the same list of words, have the student read each of the words previously spelled. To expedite this part of the lesson, the teacher may present the words on a list or on index cards. The critical learning factor is that the student read the words previously spelled after a lapse of time to transfer the knowledge gained in spelling to the task of reading the words.

If the student is having trouble reading a word, a helpful scaffold is to cover part of the word to simplify the task. For example, if the student is struggling with the word *shut*, cover part so that only the *sh* digraph is visible. After the reader pronounces /sh/, uncover the rest. This "coverup" strategy is widely applicable in helping children decode unrecognized words.

Eldredge (1995) explains an effective vowel-first blending technique that works well with letter manipulatives. First, help the reader isolate and give the sound of the vowel (e.g., the /u/ in *shut*.) Then lead the student to blend the initial consonant(s) with the vowel (e.g., /sh/u/, /shu/). Finally, help the student blend the onset-vowel chunk to any remaining consonants at the end of the word (e.g., /shu/t/, *shut*). This technique has the virtue of working with only two chunks at a time, and the particular sequence minimizes phoneme distortion to facilitate blending. Physically moving the letter manipulatives apart or together helps the student focus on the relevant chunks.

If the student is unable to read a word previously spelled, model and explain how to decode the word. Begin with the vowel, blend the initial consonant to the vowel, and blend the consonant-vowel chunk to any consonants after the vowel. Again, we have found that asking a student questions when he or she is struggling to read a word usually adds to the frustration. After working through the other words on your list, have your student return for another shot at the troublesome word.

If letterbox lessons do not lead to reading connected text, there is little likelihood that the student will apply new correspondences in ordinary reading and writing. Students will adopt decoding strategies only when they work to unlock unfamiliar written words in stories (Adams, 1990). For decoding to work, early texts must be composed of words decodable given the correspondences a student has learned (Juel & Roper/Schneider, 1985). One series that develops vowel knowledge is the Phonics Readers from Educational Insights (1990). These inexpensive books progress through short-vowel and long-vowel spellings with colorful illustrations and surprisingly engaging stories, given the constraints of vocabulary control.

Most children take pleasure in their success with well-designed letterbox lessons. They often look forward to the lesson as a game they can consistently win. However, other students may say the lesson is "boring." This probably means that the student was confused by a difficult lesson and feels frustrated. Future lessons can be salvaged by making them easier: using fewer letters, focusing on a single vowel, selecting simpler words, and reviewing the identities of the phonemes for each new correspondence. Make sure that the student is not expected to spell irregular words or use correspondences he or she hasn't learned. If the lesson is as simple as possible and the student still isn't catching on, it may be necessary to provide more basic work in phoneme awareness to help the student gain alphabetic insight (Murray, 1998).

Effectiveness of letterbox lessons

The letterbox lesson is an application of research on how children turn unfamiliar words into sight words (Ehri, 1991, 1995). Variations on the technique have helped delayed readers make dramatic reading gains (e.g., Bryant & Bradley, 1985). We have not yet conducted controlled experiments comparing the progress of students learning with letterbox lessons with that of students receiving other instruction, but we have gathered and analyzed pretest and posttest results with low achieving first graders in public schools. These students were tutored by undergraduate education majors in lessons modeled after the Reading Recovery program. Children were seen twice a week for half-hour sessions, a total of 12 meetings, to supplement their classroom work in reading. Using progress through graded word lists as a benchmark, students receiving letterbox instruction in a program of reading and writing meaningful text gained an average of 1.1 reading levels. This means, for example, that emergent readers tended to advance to preprimer levels, that primer readers tended to succeed with first-grade words, and so forth. Informally, tutors have reported that their students show great excitement and enhanced motivation for learning when they gain alphabetic insight.

The letterbox lesson at home. The letterbox lesson is ideally suited to individual tutoring because the correspondences introduced in each lesson can be tailored to the specific gaps in correspondence knowledge revealed through continual assessment. The technique holds promise for instruction with classroom groups as well. The lesson could be readily adapted by creating large-scale letterboxes and letter manipulatives for teacher explanation and modeling, and by distributing sets of letters and letterboxes for individual response.

Theresa Lesniak, an Auburn senior majoring in elementary education and the second author of this article, practiced her letterbox techniques with her two young daughters at home. She reports,

> I became a true believer in the letterbox lesson when I used it to teach my daughters to read. My 6-year-old, Samantha, could read many small words due to repetition, but had trouble decoding longer, unfamiliar words. Any word that contained a two-consonant blend, in particular *tr*, was troublesome for her. After only a few experiences using the letterbox lesson she would concentrate on all of the letters in a word. She could then sound out various unknown words by paying particular attention to each letter and the corresponding phoneme.

> Even my 4-year-old, Alex, began to decode and blend words using the method. She knew her letters and phonemes, but she would look at the first letter in a word and guess the word, instead of reading it. At the time, I felt she was too young developmentally to be able to decode and blend words. However, Alex took an interest in the letterbox lesson when she observed her older sister having fun working with letters. I decided to see if

A letterbox lesson

This transcript illustrates an early letterbox lesson that Theresa carried out with her daughter Alex, then only 4 years old.

Theresa: Today we are going to work on the /a/ sound. That's a sound of a crying baby, /aaaa/. We spell that sound with letter *a*. Okay, are you ready to spell some words?

Alex: Yep.

Theresa: (Places three letterbox sets and all the letters for the lesson in front of Alex: *c, l, m, g, f, t, p, h,* and *a*.) Okay, *hat*. She wore a lovely hat.

Alex: *Hat...hat.../h/.../h/* (places *h* in first box)...hat (places *a* in second box, then *t* in the last box). *Hat.*

Theresa: *Hat* (stressing /a/). Okay, very good. Okay, are you ready for the next word? You have to take those letters off. (Alex takes letters off the boxes.) The next word is going to be *can*.

Alex: *Can*? Okay.

Theresa: I want a can (stressing each phoneme) of soda.

Alex: (Places the *c* and *a* in first and second boxes appropriately.) Which one?

Theresa: *Can* (stressing each letter).

Alex: Which one?

Theresa: Listen to the sounds: /c/a/n/ (very slowly sounded out with extra stressing on the /n/).

Alex: *Can* (looks through the letters).

Theresa: *Cannnn.* (Alex places the /n/ in the last box) There you go, *cannnn.* Okay, are you ready for the next one?

Alex: Uh-huh.

Theresa: Okay, you gotta take those off. (Alex takes the letters off of the boxes.) *Fat.* The doggie was very fat.

Alex: *Fat.*

Theresa: *Fat.*

Alex: *Fat.../f/.../a/.../a/.../a/.../t/* (looks through letters, picks up and places *f* in first box, then *a* and *t* respectively). *Fat, fat.*

Theresa: Fat. Okay, take them off, we have to spell the next one. (The letters are removed.)

Alex: Yep.

Theresa: *Man.*

Alex: /Mmm/.

Theresa: My daddy is a man...*man* (stressing each phoneme).

Alex: (Places each letter correctly.) There.

Theresa: *Man.* Okay, the next word...you gotta take those off (the letters are removed). Okay, last word: *lap.* Come sit in my lap.

Alex: Okay (chooses correct letters and begins placing them).

Theresa: *Lap.* Come sit in my lap, and I'll read you a story. *Lap* (stressing each sound).

Alex: *Lap* (finishes places the letters). *L, a, p, lap.*

Theresa: Okay, now I'm going to put the letters out, and you have to tell me what the word is. You ready?

(continued)

A letterbox lesson (continued)

Alex:	Uh-huh.
Theresa:	Let's move these. (The boxes are moved, then the letters *c*, *a*, and *t* are placed in front of Alex.
Alex:	*Cat.*
Theresa:	Good. (The letters *c*, *a*, and *n* are placed before Alex.)
Alex:	*Can.*
Theresa:	Good. Okay, are you ready? (The letters *f*, *a*, and *t* are presented).
Alex:	*Fat?*
Theresa:	Good. Can you tell me what this says? (*Man* is spelled).
Alex:	*Man!*
Theresa:	Okay, this is a tough one. (The letters *n*, *a*, and *p* are presented. The word *nap* was not spelled earlier in the lesson. Theresa is trying to see if Alex can form a new word by sounding out letters she knows about, but has not yet used).
Alex:	(pause) /Nnn...ap/...*nap!*
Theresa:	Good. Okay, last one, then I'll let you play with the letters (*Hat* is spelled).
Alex:	*Haaat.*
Theresa:	Very good.

Theresa then selected a book, *Hop on Pop* by Dr. Seuss, and focused on the pages that contained many words similar to those Alex had spelled and read in the letterbox lesson. Alex read the simple text accurately and enjoyed the story.

---

my 4-year-old would like to try the lesson, too.

Alex and I worked on small words, such as *cat*, *man*, and *nap*. I was amazed when she began filling the boxes with the correct letters. She is by no means an expert at reading, but she does pay attention to each letter in a word and is able to decode and blend shorter words. For example, she knew the word *cat* by heart, logographically. In the past any word that started with a *c* would have been termed *cat*. After working with the letterbox lesson I placed the word *can* in front of Alex. She knew it was not *cat* and slowly sounded out each letter to find the correct word.

While Theresa's children have been exceptionally well prepared by home lit-eracy experiences, the letterbox lesson may be a practical means by which parents can provide decoding instruction for their children. The materials are inexpensive, the lesson time is brief, and the techniques can be learned without extensive training. More important, the systematic and explicit decoding instruction of the letterbox lesson can be nestled within meaningful experiences, reading storybooks, and experimenting with emergent writing.

REFERENCES

Adams, M.J. (1990). *Beginning to read: Thinking and learning about print*. Cambridge, MA: MIT Press.

Bryant, P.E., & Bradley, L. (1985). *Children's reading problems: Psychology and education*. New York: Oxford.

Delpit, L.D. (1988). The silenced dialogue: Power and pedagogy in educating other people's children. *Harvard Educational Review, 58*, 280–298.

Educational Insights. (1990). *Phonics readers*. Carson, CA, and St. Albans, Herts, England: Author.

Ehri, L.C. (1991). Development of the ability to read words. In R. Barr, M.L. Kamil, P.B. Mosenthal, & P.D. Pearson (Eds.), *Handbook of reading research, Vol. II* (pp. 383–417). White Plains, NY: Longman.

Ehri, L.C. (1995). Phases of development in learning to read words by sight. *Journal of Research in Reading, 18*, 116–125.

Eldredge, J.L. (1995). *Teaching decoding in holistic classrooms*. Englewood Cliffs, NJ: Merrill.

Fry, E. (1998). The most common phonograms. *The Reading Teacher, 51*, 620–622.

Juel, C., & Roper/Schneider, D. (1985). The influence of basal readers on first grade reading. *Reading Research Quarterly, 20*, 134–152.

Iversen, S., & Tunmer, W.E. (1993). Phonological processing skills and the Reading Recovery program. *Journal of Educational Psychology, 85*, 112–126.

Liberman, I.Y., & Liberman, A.M. (1992). Whole language versus code emphasis: Underlying assumptions and their implications for reading instruction. In P.B. Gough, L.C. Ehri, & R. Treiman (Eds.), *Reading acquisition* (pp. 343–366). Hillsdale, NJ: Erlbaum.

Murray, B.A., (1998). Gaining alphabetic insight: Is phoneme manipulation skill or identity knowledge causal? *Journal of Educational Psychology, 90*, 461–475.

Murray, B.A., Stahl, S.A., & Ivey, M.G. (1996). Developing phonological awareness through alphabet books. *Reading and Writing: An Interdisciplinary Journal, 8*, 307–322.

Opitz, M.F. (1998). Children's books to develop phonemic awareness—For you and parents, too! *The Reading Teacher, 51*, 526–527.

Pinnell, G.S., Fried, M.D., & Estice, R.M. (1990). Reading Recovery: Learning how to make a difference. *The Reading Teacher, 43*, 282–295.

Spiegel, D. (1992). Blending whole language and systematic direct instruction. *The Reading Teacher, 46*, 38–44.

Wallach, M.A., & Wallach, L. (1976). *Teaching all children to read*. Chicago: University of Chicago Press.

Yopp, H.K. (1992). Developing phonemic awareness in young children. *The Reading Teacher, 45*, 696–703.

The most common phonograms

Edward Fry

VOLUME 51, NUMBER 7, APRIL 1998

There are a lot of phonograms. In a recent study (Fry, 1998) I found 353 different phonograms (rimes or word families) that were contained in between 2 and 26 relatively common one-syllable words for each phonogram.

The teacher's problem, and the curriculum developer's problem, is which ones to teach first. One way to answer this question is to determine the phonograms that are the most common. That answer is given in the Table. The 38 most common phonograms are presented in rank order with rank being determined by the number of words in each phonogram family. Hence the phonogram family with the most words is *-ay*, which included such words as *say, day,* and *pay.*

In this study I defined phonograms or rimes as the vowel sound plus any subsequent consonants in a syllable. Single vowels without any following consonants that could be made into a word, such as /o/ in *go*, were also considered phonograms.

Why teach phonograms?

The simple answer to this question is that it helps many students to learn to read and write better. Certainly, the phonogram approach is not a complete reading or spelling program, or even a complete phonics program. But it's a definite help in decoding.

For example, Marilyn Adams (1990) states,

> As coherent psychological units in themselves, the onset and rime are relatively easy to remember and to splice back together. Yet another advantage of exploiting phonograms in decoding instruction is that they provide a means of introducing and exercising many primer words with relative efficiency and this, as we have seen, is in marked contrast to the slowness with which words can be developed through individual letter-sound correspondences. Again this advantage has long been recognized in many instructional programs. (p. 321)

Likewise, Jo Anne Vacca, Richard Vacca, and Mary Gove (1995) state,

Most common phonograms in rank order based on frequency (number of uses in monosyllabic words)*

Frequency	Rime	Example words
26	-ay	jay say pay day play
26	-ill	hill Bill will fill spill
22	-ip	ship dip tip skip trip
19	-at	cat fat bat rat sat
19	-am	ham jam dam ram Sam
19	-ag	bag rag tag wag sag
19	-ack	back sack Jack black track
19	-ank	bank sank tank blank drank
19	-ick	sick Dick pick quick chick
18	-ell	bell sell fell tell yell
18	-ot	pot not hot dot got
18	-ing	ring sing king wing thing
18	-ap	cap map tap clap trap
18	-unk	sunk junk bunk flunk skunk
17	-ail	pail jail nail sail tail
17	-ain	rain pain main chain plain
17	-eed	feed seed weed need freed
17	-y	my by dry try fly
17	-out	pout trout scout shout spout
17	-ug	rug bug hug dug tug
16	-op	mop cop pop top hop
16	-in	pin tin win chin thin
16	-an	pan man ran tan Dan
16	-est	best nest pest rest test
16	-ink	pink sink rink link drink
16	-ow	low slow grow show snow
16	-ew	new few chew grew blew
16	-ore	more sore tore store score
15	-ed	bed red fed led Ted
15	-ab	cab dab jab lab crab
15	-ob	cob job rob Bob knob
15	-ock	sock rock lock dock block
15	-ake	cake lake make take brake
15	-ine	line nine pine fine shine
14	-ight	knight light right night fight
14	-im	swim him Kim rim brim
14	-uck	duck luck suck truck buck
14	-um	gum bum hum drum plum

*For a complete list of all example words see Fry (1998).

Phonics instruction needs to include the teaching of onset and rimes. Instead of teaching phonics rules, teach children to use onsets and rimes....We can safely conclude that phonics information is much easier for young readers to acquire when phonograms are taught than when a one-on-one blending process is taught. (p. 287)

Utility of phonograms

I found that just 38 phonograms with added beginning consonants can make 654 different one-syllable words. These same phonograms can be found in many polysyllabic words as well. This finding is basically in harmony with an earlier study by Wylie and Durrell (in Vacca, Vacca, & Gove, 1995) that found that 37 phonograms could form nearly 500 primary-grade words.

In my study I went completely through two rhyming dictionaries (Alee, 1983; Webster, 1987) and one dissertation on the topic (Stanback, 1991), as a cross check, and selected all relatively common example words. All of the 353 phonograms and their several thousand example words fill a small book (Fry, 1998). This article presents the most useful of those 353 rhymes.

Teaching phonograms

There are numerous ways to teach phonograms or extend reading and spelling vocabulary by using them.

The phonograms are incorporated in many basal reading series, phonics systems, reading readiness lessons, and spelling series that are produced by commercial publishers.

Teacher-made materials can also be used. These include making word charts, word wheels, games, slip charts, or individual cards (onset on one card and rime on another—students match and blend).

When a student attacks an unknown word, or the teacher introduces a new word in reading or spelling, the teacher shows the similar pattern in a known word.

Special spelling lessons using word lists focusing on just one or two patterns can also be effective.

Conclusion

With just 38 rimes students can write, spell, or read over 600 relatively common one-syllable words. This is one reason to use the phonograms in the Table for reading and spelling lessons. These words suggest an important part of an effective beginning reading curriculum.

REFERENCES

Adams, M.J. (1990). *Beginning to read.* Cambridge, MA: MIT Press.

Alee, J.G. (1983). Rhyming dictionary. In *Webster's encyclopedia of dictionaries.* Baltimore, MD: Ottenheimer.

Fry, E. (1998). *Phonics patterns: Onset and rhyme word lists.* Laguna Beach, CA: Laguna Beach Educational Books.

Stanback, M.L. (1991). *Syllable and rime patterns for teaching reading: Analysis of a frequency based vocabulary of 17,602 words.* Unpublished doctoral dissertation.

Teachers College, Columbia University, New York.

Vacca, J.L., Vacca, R.T., & Gove, M.K. (1995). *Reading and learning to read.* New York: HarperCollins.

Webster's compact rhyming dictionary. (1987). Springfield, MA: Merriam-Webster.

The flashcard strikes back

Tom Nicholson

VOLUME 52, NUMBER 2, OCTOBER 1998

Flashcards have a terrible reputation (McCullough, 1955). But it's undeserved. They are a very direct way of teaching children to read words quickly, especially words that are very frequent in stories, yet are irregular in their spellings (e.g., words like *after, because, come, one, put, there, would*). Although it is extremely important for beginning and struggling readers to be taught phonemic awareness and some basic phonics skills so they can sound out simple, regular words like *cat* (Nicholson, 1994, 1997), this is not enough for them to read stories. To read stories, they have to be able to identify high-frequency, irregularly spelled glue words. Flashcards can help them to build knowledge of these high-frequency words, which have to be known if children are to bootstrap themselves into reading of text.

Does reading words faster matter?

Anyone who has listened to unskilled readers stumbling along the page, making lots of mistakes, knows that their comprehension of what they read is likely to be shattered by the amount of cognitive effort that is being diverted to the task of saying words. If these children were able to read quickly and accurately, then the extra mental energy saved by not having to struggle with each word could be applied to comprehending what they read, which is what reading is all about.

Good readers read words quickly and effortlessly. They have automatic word reading skills. Thus, they can devote their full mental energies to comprehension. Flashcards can foster automaticity by helping children to read words accurately and quickly. Critics argue that flashcards only teach children to "bark" at print and do not contribute to the bottom line of reading, which is comprehension. But recent research suggests the opposite, that teaching children to read words faster can improve reading comprehension dramatically (Tan & Nicholson, 1997).

All sophisticated performances require the ability to orchestrate a variety of skills. Reading is no exception. To combine several skills at once, some of them have to be overlearned. Overlearning applies to everyday skills as well as specialist skills. Bloom (1986) gives the example of walking. Watching a 1-year-old who has just started to walk reminds us that the everyday skills we take for granted have to be practised and overlearned. One-year-olds look where they are walking, adjust their pace, and so on. If they lose concentration, they are likely to fall on their face. Success in sport also requires automaticity of skills. When you watch a novice roller-blader, wearing all kinds of protective gear, stumbling along, staring intently at the ground, and looking highly unstable, it is obvious that a number of skating subskills need to be automatized before that person is going to enjoy the sport. In the same way, once a child can read words effortlessly, his or her mind is then free to concentrate on enjoying the content of what is being read.

When you have achieved automaticity of word reading, the skills of reading are so effortless that they are hard to control. For example, while driving it is very difficult not to read signs and other written material like billboards, and personalised licence plates, which are modern-day flashcards, with phrases like "go-4-it" or single words like *miaow* or *woof* on them.

Teaching implications

The instructional ideal is to get unskilled readers to the point where they can recognise many words with ease, so that they can start reading stories independently. Flashcards can help the child achieve this goal. And flashcards are simple to make. All you need is the humble felt pen, scissors, and cardboard. You can even ask the better readers in your class to make some for you, but be sure to check their spelling, or insist that they do a dictionary check. You don't want them to create a list like LOOOK, TAYBUL, NIFE, SPUNE, and so on. Although invented spellings can be acceptable in children's own writing, it is unproductive to use them for teaching children to read. It is better that children see the flashcard words as they are actually spelled in published books. Thus, when they come to read the correct spellings, such as LOOK, TABLE, KNIFE, and SPOON in their stories and textbooks, they will not be confused.

You can use flashcards as a scaffolding technique, so that unskilled readers can read and get meaning from stories that are otherwise too difficult. Tan and Nicholson (1997) found that a short session of flashcard training (say, 20 minutes), with 20 difficult words from a 200-word story, set up a below-average reader for a positive reading experience. In their study, they compared three matched groups of unskilled readers, aged from 7 to 10 years. Two of the matched groups received flashcard training, either with one-word flashcards or sentence flashcards. The third group, a control group, discussed the flashcard words verbally but did not read them. The researchers ensured that all children in the study understood the meanings of the words. There was no point in training children to read words quickly if they did not understand them. Here were the results for flashcard speed and reading comprehension:

• Speed of flashcard reading (words per minute): One-word = 54 wpm, Sentence = 65 wpm, Control = 26 wpm

• Comprehension questions correct: One-word = 74%, Sentence = 80%, Control = 42%

• Passage recall (main ideas and details): One-word = 54%, Sentence = 53%, Control = 30%

Overall, the results showed no significant differences between the two flashcard training groups (one-word versus sentence) in terms of speed of word reading or reading comprehension. Yet the flashcard training groups were significantly better than the control group, both for speed of reading flashcard words, and for reading comprehension. The results showed that although all the children in the study knew what the flashcard words meant, it was only the children who were trained to read words quickly who improved their speed and their comprehension. It is also interesting to note that 100% of the children who received the flashcard training said that they enjoyed their lessons. Flashcards can be fun.

Here is a specific example of how to do the same kind of training they did. Locate a story that is suitable for the children you teach. For example, let's choose *When the Moon Was Blue* (Cowley, 1989), which is for beginning readers. It contains about 200 words. Select 10% of the words (i.e., 20 words) for training, glue words, and other words you feel will present some difficulty. Put the words on separate flashcards. You can use either single-word flashcards (e.g., *raspberry*) or sentence flashcards to provide the child

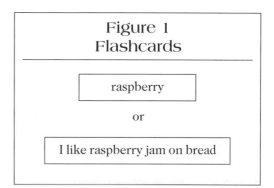

Figure 1
Flashcards

raspberry

or

I like raspberry jam on bread

with some context (e.g., "I like *raspberry* jam on bread"). See Figure 1.

Tan and Nicholson (1997) found no difference between either type of flashcard in terms of effectiveness. It's a matter of personal preference. Present each of the 20 flashcards, one by one. See if the children can recognise them. If not, pronounce the words for the children. Also check to see if the meaning of each word is understood. If you are using single-word flashcards, write a phrase on the back of the card (e.g., "raspberry jam"). If the children do not know what the word means, turn around the card and show the phrase. Ask the children to use the word in a sentence as well. Be sure that they have a good understanding of the word.

I like to use sentence flashcards. Why? They are more interesting. And I use flashcard sentences that are NOT from the story. Why? It's more interesting if you do not give the child extra cues as to the meaning of the story. Otherwise, they can easily guess the plot. It's more fun to keep it a surprise. Also, by training a child with different sentence contexts, you are hoping they will be able to transfer from flashcard contexts to the same words in new contexts. This, after all, is what the training is designed to do. You want the child to be able to read the same word in many sentence contexts.

As you present each flashcard, point to the difficult word, so that the child knows this is the one you are focusing on. For example, the story *When the Moon Was Blue* contains words like *lemonade, raspberry, golden, fantastic,* and *terrible*. Discuss the meanings of the words as you run through the flashcards on the first practice. Also, on the first practice, encourage the child to sound out each word, using the moving-thumb technique of slowly moving your thumb across the word in bits (e.g., "lem-on-ade"). Another technique, for children who are unable to recognize long words, is to teach them to read just the first three letters (e.g., *lem* in *lemonade*). This strategy makes a long word accessible. I find that poor readers especially can often come up with the correct word by using this simple first-three-letters strategy. Both strategies (moving thumb and first-three-letters) have the added advantage of signalling that it is OK for the child to use emerging phonics skills to pronounce these words. This is much preferable to reliance on using unhelpful distinctive cues to recognise words (e.g., smudge marks on the flashcards, or the "tail" on the word *dog*).

Once the flashcards are well learned and can be read quickly, ask the pupil to guess what the story will be about, just from the flashcard words. Children are rarely able to guess the real plot of the story, but it's a good way of building up risk taking and curiosity about the story. They can come up with some very funny predictions of what the story will be about. If you are working with a single child, it's a good idea to let the child do his or her own self-training with the flashcards. As the self-training proceeds, the child can put the easy cards to one side and continue working on the difficult cards. Be sure to check that the child is reading each flashcard correctly. At the end of 20 minutes (don't go overtime), go straight to reading the story. Here is a sample page (Cowley, 1989):

> When the moon was blue...
> The sea was made of lemonade
> And my boat was a raspberry bun.

After the child reads the story aloud to you, ask him or her to answer some questions or else retell the story. Tan and Nicholson (1997) found that reading accuracy, speed, and comprehension were much improved if children received one-word or sentence flashcard training before they read the story.

In another study, Taka (1997) obtained similar results, using flashcards as part of a bingo game, with a small group of adult literacy learners. The bingo card had 25 squares, with each square containing one of the 25 words to be learned. The tutor shuffled the pile of 25 flashcards and started reading them out. Students had to find the called-out word on the bingo card, and place a button in the right square on the card. When a student completed a row, column, or diagonal of five words, they called out "bingo." After a quick check by the group to verify that the student had indeed located the correct words, a new game began. The adults improved in word reading accuracy as a result of the bingo game training, and the training had a positive effect on their reading comprehension when they read stories that contained the trained words. It's surprising how this simple technique of using flashcards can make a difficult-to-read story more accessible to poor readers. Taka (1997) reported that the adult learners really enjoyed the bingo games. They thought of songs or phrases to help them get the meaning of each trained word (e.g., "I *found* my thrill on blueberry hill," "I just *called* to say I love you," for the words *found* and *called*).

To consolidate learning of glue words, I like to use a *First Dictionary Card* (Fepulea'i, 1993), or something similar, with about 80 high-frequency words on it (e.g., *was, come, of*), as well as 20 or so interest words (e.g., *mother, cousin, grandad*). This card is normally used as a spelling resource to help beginners with their story writing, but it can also be used to practise children's word reading of highly frequent, yet irregularly spelled glue words (see Figure 2).

If you want to make your own First Dictionary Card, a list of the first 100 very frequent words is included in *A New Zealand Basic Word List* (Elley, Croft, & Cowie, 1997). Another source is *The American Heritage Word Frequency Book* (Carroll, 1971), which also includes the most frequent 100 words. The First Dictionary Card can be used as a megaflashcard for teaching children to read words faster. This First Dictionary Card is laminated, which enables the student to use a felt pen to circle and mark words during instruction. Spending 10 minutes each day practising words on a dictionary card can be a lot of fun, as the child aims for accuracy and speed of reading. In addition, the card is immediately available at each pupil's desk as a simple dictionary resource when writing stories.

I also take advantage of the First Dictionary Card to practise spelling accuracy. I pick words randomly from the card, and I have the child write them or spell them aloud. Children enjoy this task, especially once they start to get a good grasp of how to spell these irregular words. As their spellings get closer and closer to the correct spelling, they will get terribly involved in the challenge of the task. I find that the training spills over into their writing. Their spellings become more readable. In my experience, it's important to practise both reading and spelling of these glue words. The different kinds of practice tend to reinforce one another. When a child's spelling starts to improve he or she feels better about writing stories, and the teacher can see the improvement.

Another technique is to use word-family flashcards, such as the Rhyme and Analogy card games (Goswami, 1995). This package has lots of rhyming flashcards like *cot, dot, ball, wall*, and so on. As children develop mastery over certain rhymes, the cards can be shuffled, so that the families get mixed up. Children can also read them as doubles, to practise reading compounds. The compounds do not have to make sense, since children are just

Figure 2
First Dictionary Card example

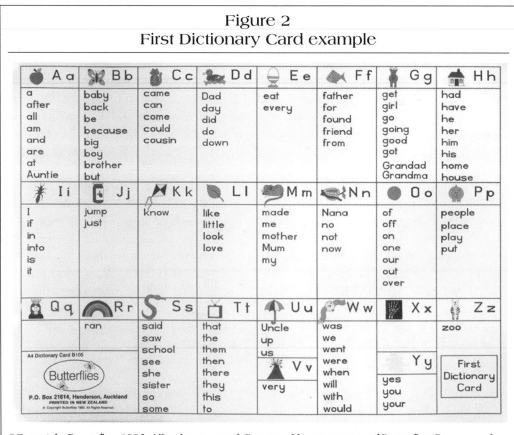

🍎 A a	🦋 B b	🍍 C c	🦆 D d	🥚 E e	🐟 F f	🦌 G g	🏠 H h
a	baby	came	Dad	eat	father	get	had
after	back	can	day	every	for	girl	have
all	be	come	did		found	go	he
am	because	could	do		friend	going	her
and	big	cousin	down		from	good	him
are	boy					got	his
at	brother					Grandad	home
Auntie	but					Grandma	house

🐜 I i	🧃 J j	🪁 K k	🍃 L l	🪱 M m	🐢 N n	⚫ O o	🧅 P p
I	jump	know	like	made	Nana	of	people
if	just		little	me	no	off	place
in			look	mother	not	on	play
into			love	Mum	now	one	put
is				my		our	
it						out	
						over	

👑 Q q	🌈 R r	🐍 S s	🔲 T t	☂️ U u	🐛 W w	✨ X x	🦓 Z z
	ran	said	that	Uncle	was		zoo
		saw	the	up	we		
		school	them	us	went		
		see	then		were	**Y y**	
		she	there	**V v**	when	yes	**First Dictionary Card**
		sister	they		will	you	
		so	this	very	with	your	
		some	to		would		

A4 Dictionary Card B105

Butterflies

P.O. Box 21614, Henderson, Auckland
PRINTED IN NEW ZEALAND
© Copyright Butterflies 1993. All Rights Reserved.

playing with possible words (e.g., *froghat, dogmat*). I find that these flashcard sessions are excellent for practising simple phonics skills. Flashcards are useful for training children to read regularly spelled words as well as the irregular, glue words.

I always follow up flashcard practice with some reading, making sure that the story or article is challenging, but achievable. After reading the story, I may ask the pupil to write a summary of the story. If he or she is a poor reader, I ask for only five sentences. After writing the summary, the child corrects misspellings of words in the summary that are found on their First Dictionary Card. For other misspellings, I ask them to use a slightly more extensive dictionary, such as *My Words* (Croft, 1989) or *Spiral Dictionary* (Fepulea'i, 1997), which have about 300 high-frequency words. For better readers, I use *Spell-Write* (Croft, 1998), which has a list of 3,500 often-used words. If the child is a very poor reader, I make the corrections myself, usually correcting only the worst mistakes, those that I can't read myself. These follow-up activities are very important, because they send the message to the child that skills training has practical application to the realities of reading and writing.

The flashcard of the future

It would be a shame if teachers read this article and thought that it was a call to dig into the broom cupboards and find all those 1950s flashcards. We do not want children to be mindlessly drilled by flashcard junkies. But flashcards can be a useful technique if used properly. Teachers need to be aware of the dangers of drill and skill in turning children off reading altogether. But we also have to acknowledge that many children do not read fluently for their age (Pinnell, Pikulski, Wixson, Campbell, Gough, & Beatty, 1995). Flashcards can promote fluency and in turn help reading comprehension. And they can be a lot of fun.

For a poor reader especially, there is something reassuring about being good at one skill of reading, just as there is a feeling of satisfaction about hitting a consistent golf shot, even if it's only when you are at practice. Flashcards can strike back. They can make a poor reader a better reader. The key to success is to use flashcards sensibly, in small doses, for fun, and with pizzazz!

REFERENCES

Bloom, B.S. (1986). Automaticity. *Educational Leadership, 43*, 70–77.

Carroll, J.B. (1971). *American Heritage word frequency book*. Boston: Houghton Mifflin.

Cowley, J. (1989). *When the moon was blue*. Crystal Lake, IL: Rigby.

Croft, C. (1998). *Spell-write*. Auckland, New Zealand: New Zealand Council for Educational Research.

Croft, C. (1989). *My words*. Auckland, New Zealand: New Zealand Council for Educational Research.

Elley, W.B., Croft, C., & Cowie, C. (1977). *A New Zealand basic word list. Revision of the Dolch basic sight vocabulary list*. Wellington, New Zealand: New Zealand Council for Educational Research.

Fepulea'i, H. (1993). *First dictionary card*. Auckland, New Zealand: Butterflies (Resources for Young Learners).

Fepulea'i, H. (1997). *Spiral dictionary*. Auckland, New Zealand: Butterflies (Resources for Young Learners).

Goswami, U. (Ed.). (1995). *Rhyme and analogy card games*. Oxford, UK: Oxford University Press.

McCullough, C. (1955). Flash cards—The opiate of the reading program? *Elementary English, 32*, 379–381.

Nicholson, T. (1994). *At the cutting edge: Recent research on learning to read and spell*. Wellington, New Zealand: New Zealand Council for Educational Research.

Nicholson, T. (1997). *Solving reading problems*. Wellington, New Zealand: New Zealand Council for Educational Research.

Pinnell, G.S., Pikulski, J.J., Wixson, K.K., Campbell, J.R., Gough, P.B., & Beatty, A.S. (1995). *Listening to children read aloud: Data from NAEP's integrated reading performance record (IRPR) at grade 4*. Washington, DC: National Center for Education Statistics.

Taka, M.L. (1997). *Word game bingo and adult literacy students. Sight word acquisition and reading comprehension.* Unpublished master's thesis, The University of Auckland, Auckland, New Zealand.

Tan, A., & Nicholson, T. (1997). Flashcards revisited: Training poor readers to read words faster improves their comprehension of text. *Journal of Educational Psychology, 89,* 276–288.

Footprints on the classroom wall

Mary Gorman

VOLUME 47, NUMBER 2, OCTOBER 1993

Should students be allowed to put footprints on the wall? Students at one Ohio elementary school are encouraged to put footprints on the floor and wall as they learn to read, write, and spell basic words.

As third graders entered the Reading Center, they were greeted with a set of paper footprints mounted on the floor. A basic sight word was printed on each. Words were selected to develop meaningful sentences. *Come and read with me. Did you know reading could be fun?*

The footprints for each sentence were left on the floor for one week. Each day the children walked alongside the footprints as they read the words. Then they attempted to write the entire sentence. Misspelled words were corrected, and students rewrote the sentence correctly. This procedure was followed for 4 days. On Friday of each week, the students wrote the sentence from dictation and were usually pleased with their accomplishments.

When a new sentence was presented, the previous sentence was removed and mounted on the wall for later review. Sentences were constructed to include statements, questions, and exclamations. The children were exposed to the various types of sentences and the punctuation needed for each type.

Evidence of our success was noted when *with* was no longer spelled *whith* and *want* was no longer spelled *wont*. Other examples of success became evident with the words *when*, which previously had been spelled *wen*, *was* previously *wus*, and *get* previously *git*.

In addition, students commented that they had remembered to begin each sentence with a capital letter and to use the correct punctuation at the end. Both teacher and students were pleased with the success of our experiential project.

Sentencing: The psycholinguistic guessing game

Ann K. Hall

VOLUME 49, NUMBER 1, SEPTEMBER 1995

In an article that has greatly influenced our understanding of the reading process, Kenneth Goodman (1976) called reading a "psycholinguistic guessing game." According to Goodman, reading requires the reader to combine cognitive (knowledge/reasoning) and linguistic (language) abilities to predict words, using minimal graphophonic (letter/sound) cues. Goodman argued that since students must learn to play the psycholinguistic guessing game as they develop reading ability, effective methods and materials must be used by teachers who understand the rules of the game. Readers must be helped to select the most productive cues, using their knowledge of language structure and drawing on their experiences and concepts. The ability to anticipate that which has not been seen is vital in reading.

With these thoughts in mind and with fond memories of playing Hangman, I developed Sentencing as a means of introducing my undergraduate elementary education students to the various cueing systems available to readers. As they played in teams and shared their thoughts ("It can't be *are* because you need a singular verb," "After the comma it must be *although* or *however*"), there was a serendipitous occurrence—what a wonderful way to introduce my preservice teachers to the concept of metacognition!

These preservice students went on to intern in the schools, and they played the game with their students. The first report was, "My students (sixth graders) loved it, and my cooperating teacher really enjoyed it." We discovered that Sentencing can be played with students from third grade through high school; but with all levels, a few practice rounds are needed. It takes only about 5 minutes to play one sentence.

Sentencing challenges students to use syntactic and semantic cues while reconstructing a sentence which is made by a teacher or that comes from an appropriate text. It encourages players to use and share strategies based on their metacognitive knowledge, and it allows the teacher to observe the strategies being used.

Materials needed:

1. Sentences of 7–15 words appropriate for all players' reading levels. Use sentences with strong syntax and sufficient meaning load. Do not include proper nouns or contractions. Here are some examples of appropriate sentences to use:

> This afternoon we played softball, and my team won.
> If you are warm, feel free to take your jacket off.
> It has been raining for days, and I am getting tired of it.

2. Two "free letter" cards for each team. These cards will allow players to guess the first letter of a word as needed during the game.

How to play:

Explain rules as you play a practice round.

1. Divide the class into two or three teams (3–8 students per team).

2. Present a sentence to players as shown in Figure 1. Reveal only one key word (such as *homework* in the figure) to clue students in to the schema needed.

3. Call attention to any clues such as punctuation.

4. Pick a team to go first (make sure teams take turns going first). Have each team choose a spokesperson to gather input from team members and to speak for the team. Ask the team going first the number of the word they would like revealed. Always reveal one word of the team's choice at the beginning of each team's turn, unless there is only one word remaining.

5. Upon your revelation of a word, the team has two choices:

a. Guess another word in the sentence. If the players are correct, they get two points and continue their turn.

b. Use a "free letter" card. Players can ask you to write the first letter of any word they choose. After seeing the letter, they must attempt to guess any of the words. If they are correct, they receive one point. A "free letter" card may also be used for the second letter of a word if the first letter has already been revealed, and so on. Guessing a word with one or more letters revealed also earns one point.

6. Play goes to the next team when a team makes an incorrect guess. Players have one word of the sentence revealed and then either guess a word or use a free letter card. If they guess incorrectly, it's the next team's turn.

7. Inform the teams that you cannot reveal the last word remaining in a sentence.

8. Play is over when the entire sentence is guessed.

9. Tally the score for each team.

Figure 1			
1	2	3	4
5	homework 6		7
8	9	10	11

An example

Team One asks for word 1 to be revealed from the sentence in Figure 1. It is the word *I*. After group discussion the spokesperson guesses that word 5 is *my*. This guess is correct. The teacher writes in *my* and Team One receives two points. Team One players now have two options. They may guess another word or use a free letter card. They choose to ask for the first letter of word 2. The teacher writes in *n*. The board looks like Figure 2.

Team One guesses that word 2 is *never*. Their guess is incorrect, so play moves to Team Two.

Team Two asks that word 11 be revealed. The teacher writes in *play*. Team Two then guesses that word 2 is *need*. They receive 1 point for the correct answer since a letter had been revealed. They then correctly guess that word 3 is *to*, for which they receive 2 points. The team decides to use a free letter card and asks for the first letter in word 7. The teacher reveals *b*. They incorrectly guess *because*, and play returns to Team One.

Team One asks that word 10 be revealed. It is *go*. They then receive 1 point for guessing that word 7 is *before*. After good discussion they guess that word 8 is *I*, but it is not. The teacher hears, "I told you it was *we*." The board now reveals the clues shown in Figure 3.

Play continues. If you were playing, what would you do? More importantly, what are you thinking?

Here are some suggestions for teachers playing the Sentencing game:

• Play a few practice rounds to allow students to become familiar with the game before keeping score.

• Try to keep the atmosphere noncompetitive even though you keep score.

• Play a designated number of sentences once you begin scoring. Make sure teams have an equal number of chances to go first.

• Do not set a time limit for each team's turn, but encourage them to answer in a reasonable amount of time.

At first your role will be a combination of Vanna White, Alex Trebek, and a member of the Family Feud responding, "Good answer!" When you're not encouraging students, listen so you can assess the strategies they are using. However, it won't be long before one of the students

Figure 2			
I	n	to	
1	2	3	4
my	homework		
5	6		7
			.
8	9	10	11

Figure 3			
I	need	to	
1	2	3	4
my	homework		before
5	6		7
		go	play .
8	9	10	11

can take over your role and the students will be able to play on their own.

This psycholinguistic guessing game provides an enjoyable way to develop students' abilities to use semantic, syntactic, and graphophonic cues. It also provides a window through which teachers can view the metacognitive strategies of their students. Move over, Hangman, Sentencing is here!

REFERENCES

Goodman, K. (1976). Reading: A psycholinguistic guessing game. In H. Singer & R.B. Ruddell (Eds.), *Theoretical models and processes of reading* (2nd ed., pp. 497–508). Newark, DE: International Reading Association.

Monitoring spelling development

Christopher C. Hayward

VOLUME 51, NUMBER 5, FEBRUARY 1998

Here's how I devised a simple table that allows me not only to monitor my class's spelling development but also to use the information from the table to plan spelling instruction.

Teachers in our school district have devised spelling lists of high-frequency words for students at each grade level to master. During the first-grade year, each student is expected to master the conventional spelling of 30 words. The students learn these conventional spellings through authentic experiences rather than spelling tests. These experiences include using the words in their daily writing, along with guided reading and independent reading. Although the use of invented spelling is encouraged with first graders, the children are expected to master specific words from the list as the year progresses.

To assist students in valuing the importance of correct spelling, the high-frequency and important words are listed on a word wall. The word wall is made up of 26 pieces of paper designating the letters of the alphabet. I list words that the children and I decide should be included under each letter. For example, a student, the teacher, or the class may feel that the word *love* is used frequently and should be included. Gradually more words are added throughout the year as readiness for the high-frequency words increases. Once a word is listed on the wall, the students understand that it is to be spelled correctly in their writing. Through such a process, they begin to learn to use resources to help them move toward spelling mastery.

Monitoring the rates of mastery of these words has long been a frustrating problem for me. Therefore, I created a table to assist me in the monitoring of progress and to use as a guide for further instruction. The Table shows the format I used to create my spelling monitor table. It allows me to provide monthly data to parents interested in learning about their child's developmental progress in spelling.

Using a computer-generated spreadsheet, I label each of 23 rows with the names of my children. Under each name, I list the 30 high-frequency spelling words that they are expected to learn. The end product is a 23- by 30-cell spreadsheet. Once I print the spreadsheet, I am able to use it daily in my classroom.

Spelling monitor table

Antonio	Elizabeth	Bishop	Ciara	Reggie	Robert	Max	Calvin	John	Kashay	David	Ayla	Haley	Natalie	Susanna
the	the	the	the	the	the	the	the	the	the	the	the	the	the	the
and	and	and	and	and	and	and	and	and	and	and	and	and	and	and
to	to	to	to	to	to	to	to	to	to	to	to	to	to	to
is	is	is	is	is	is	is	is	is	is	is	is	is	is	is
in	in	in	in	in	in	in	in	in	in	in	in	in	in	in
it	it	it	it	it	it	it	it	it	it	it	it	it	it	it
you	you	you	you	you	you	you	you	you	you	you	you	you	you	you
he	he	he	he	he	he	he	he	he	he	he	he	he	he	he
she	she	she	she	she	she	she	she	she	she	she	she	she	she	she
at	at	at	at	at	at	at	at	at	at	at	at	at	at	at
had	had	had	had	had	had	had	had	had	had	had	had	had	had	had
has	has	has	has	has	has	has	has	has	has	has	has	has	has	has
have	have	have	have	have	have	have	have	have	have	have	have	have	have	have
by	by	by	by	by	by	by	by	by	by	by	by	by	by	by
my	my	my	my	my	my	my	my	my	my	my	my	my	my	my
me	me	me	me	me	me	me	me	me	me	me	me	me	me	me
like	like	like	like	like	like	like	like	like	like	like	like	like	like	like
love	love	love	love	love	love	love	love	love	love	love	love	love	love	love
can	can	can	can	can	can	can	can	can	can	can	can	can	can	can
go	go	go	go	go	go	go	go	go	go	go	go	go	go	go
no	no	no	no	no	no	no	no	no	no	no	no	no	no	no
yes	yes	yes	yes	yes	yes	yes	yes	yes	yes	yes	yes	yes	yes	yes
up	up	up	up	up	up	up	up	up	up	up	up	up	up	up
out	out	out	out	out	out	out	out	out	out	out	out	out	out	out
all	all	all	all	all	all	all	all	all	all	all	all	all	all	all
day	day	day	day	day	day	day	day	day	day	day	day	day	day	day
see	see	see	see	see	see	see	see	see	see	see	see	see	see	see
not	not	not	not	not	not	not	not	not	not	not	not	not	not	not
of	of	of	of	of	of	of	of	of	of	of	of	of	of	of
was	was	was	was	was	was	was	was	was	was	was	was	was	was	was

At the beginning of every month I assess my students on the 30 words without the aid of the word wall or environmental print. I emphasize to the children that this is not a "test" and it doesn't really matter if they know all or none of the words as long as they do their best. I tell the class that I am simply trying to get information to help me do a better job of teaching them how to spell. I want the total experience to be as nonthreatening as possible.

When a student spells a word correctly on one of the monthly checks it is highlighted in yellow. As the year progresses, the number of yellow squares below each name increases. A quick glance enables me to see which words the student has mastered and which still need to be targeted for further individual instruction. Looking horizontally at the rows, a large number of white spaces would indicate more instruction is needed for the whole class during reading groups, shared reading, and writing.

Such a table, combined with a nonthreatening environment and a solid instructional program, guides me in supporting each student to become a proficient speller.

Spelling for readers and writers

Jill E. Scott

Volume 48, Number 2, October 1994

Spelling instruction needs to be more meaningful for students. We don't want children to think of spelling as word lists and tests, but as a tool to enable them to express themselves in writing. Skill in spelling should be developed in context in order to achieve some meaningful purpose, not as an end in itself (Buchanan, 1989). At the same time, Adams (1990) notes that encouraging students to spell words correctly is important. Spelling must not be disregarded. However, our goal should not be for students to spell words correctly on a weekly spelling test, but rather to create competent and independent spellers and writers (Wilde, 1990).

Students progress as spellers when teachers support them as readers and writers (Bartch, 1992). Reading should be the backbone of spelling instruction. Many things we do to assist beginning literacy help spelling as well (Fehring & Thomas, 1989), such as reading familiar poems and songs on charts, reading big books, writing and reading chart stories—anything where the child is attending to print can help spelling awareness. Griffith (1991) says, "Specific incidents in which the child fo-

cuses on the spoken and written word simultaneously may enhance the acquisition of the spellings of phonemes and of whole words" (p. 232).

Griffith also mentions that text which plays with language and uses rhyme, alliteration, and patterns can focus children's attention on words and their spellings. Pointing out word and letter patterns while reading to children can also help their spelling awareness and enable them to notice patterns in words they read and words they attempt to write. Then, as children progress toward mature spelling, they learn to rely more and more on visual information rather than sound and are able to reject spellings as "not looking right" (Fehring & Thomas, 1989, p. 6). Extensive reading enables the students to develop this insight and to make it a habit.

Reading may be the backbone of informal spelling instruction, but writing is the lifeblood. Correct spelling used to be considered essential before young students began any story writing. Now we learn that "standard spelling is the consequence of writing and reading, not the access to it" (Bean & Bouffler, 1991, p. 47). Good spellers form an early consciousness of spelling through meaningful writing (Gentry, 1987). Students will learn how to spell and will learn the value of correct spelling, if they write often for authentic purposes. Examples of activities might include class newspapers or newsletters, published books, pen pal letters, thank you notes, invitations, displays in the hallway, and class books shared with other classes.

Another characteristic of a successful spelling program is the encouragement of risk taking. Spelling is a gradual process that develops through trial and error, and the best way to teach spelling is to give students freedom to take risks in their writing (Gentry, 1987). When children are in a supportive classroom with an encouraging teacher, risk taking will occur. Children will invent their own spellings. It is important to know that invented spelling is not a synonym for misspelling. "Invention is not a failure to achieve convention, but a step on the road to reaching it" (Wilde, 1992, p. 3). Gentry (1987) mentions that when students invent spellings, they are thinking and learning about words. Emergent spellers need to invent because it makes them attend to letters, sounds, and words. Adams (1990) states that "classroom encouragement of invented spellings is a promising approach toward the development of phonemic awareness and knowledge of spelling patterns" (p. 126).

A child's attitude toward spelling is also important to consider. "Beginning spellers are learning not only how to spell—they are learning an attitude towards spelling" (Fehring & Thomas, 1989,

p. 14). A classroom that treats words and spelling as interesting and enjoyable can only be an advantage to the student. When risk taking and invented spelling are treated as natural and desirable, the students will write more and thus become more knowledgeable about words.

Described below are some specific instructional activities that can be used in the classroom to enhance students' knowledge of words and spelling within a context of reading and writing.

Teacher modeling. It is important to show children how an adult figures out how to spell a word. Teachers need to model using a dictionary or other reference to look up a word, stretching out the sounds of a word to help spell it, and asking others in the classroom for assistance.

Morning message. Write a message on the chalkboard each morning pertaining to the day's activities. Discuss the conventions of the message, including the spelling.

Labels and signs. Put labels on things around the classroom such as furniture, bulletin boards, student work that is displayed, and anything else the students may want to refer to for help with spelling.

Wall charts. Post charts in the classroom with common words students may need to spell, such as family words, holiday words, or animal names.

Pattern charts. Post charts in the classroom that display spelling or phonics patterns (Butler & Turbill, 1987). Examples of onset patterns include *gr—green Greg grow grumpy agree*; b*ack*, s*ack*, t*ack* are 3 examples of the *ack* rime. Sticky notes can then be available for the children to add more words that fit the pattern as they find them in their reading. These words can then be checked before being added permanently to the list (Routman, 1991).

Spelling big book. Pattern and wall charts can be collected together into a class spelling big book to be used as a reference (Routman, 1991).

Journals. Students can write daily in journals on topics of their own choosing. Invented spelling is encouraged as students learn to take risks and use their increasing store of word and spelling knowledge.

Conferences. A very effective way to encourage standard spelling is to discuss it one-on-one with a student during a conference. Reading conferences take place after a child has read a book and discusses it with the teacher, or after a child reads a short section aloud to the teacher. Words and spellings can be highlighted and discussed. Writing conferences occur when a child has chosen to publish a piece from his or her writing. Editing occurs at this time. Conferences allow the teacher to see a child's spelling need and meet it (Calkins, 1986; Graves, 1983).

Proofreading and publishing. Perhaps the crux of a successful spelling program is to teach students how to proofread their own writing for ultimate publication. Invented spelling is a convenience for the writer, and as children write for authentic purposes, they learn that standard spelling is a courtesy to the reader (Wilde, 1992). Some specific strategies to teach proofreading are (1) Instead of circling misspelled words on stu-

dents' papers, mention the number of misspellings there are and have the students find them on their own (Wilde, 1992). (2) Proofreading is different from reading in that it requires the student to focus in on each word individually. Bean and Bouffler (1991) suggest using a ruler to uncover one word at a time. (3) Routman (1991) encourages students to look at the word and ask themselves if the word looks right. If not, what part looks wrong? Then the student should make another attempt at spelling the word.

Have-a-go. Routman (1991) describes in detail how children can use Have-a-go sheets (originally from Australia) to develop their spelling and proofreading habits. For example, students choose three words from their writing they think may be misspelled. Then they write each word three more times, changing the spelling each time, until they feel the spelling is right. Adults spell this way, oftentimes writing a word several ways on a piece of scratch paper, seeing which one looks right. This is a strategy that can help students as well. The student's Have-a-go sheet may be discussed during a conference, or a teacher may confirm the spelling for the student. An adaptation that works well with emergent spellers has the following headings: *My try, Help from a friend, Help from the teacher.*

Interesting words. We should help students appreciate the many interesting words and word families in the English language. We can call their attention to such things as interesting compound words, family words (such as *handbag*, *handball, handy, handkerchief, handshake*), and word histories.

Words within words. Looking at word parts as they fit into whole words can help children learn spelling patterns. Example: In the word *teacher* we can find *tea, each, her, teach, he,* and *ache*. Words can also be rearranged to make new words. *Star* can be rearranged to make *arts, tars,* and *rats*. These activities are better than sorting scrambled words because the students do not see incorrect letter patterns (Fehring & Thomas, 1989).

Word sorts. Give each child some word cards. For emergent spellers use words such as *bat, mat, man, can, fan, came, same, name, lip, trip, slip*. Children are then asked to sort the words into pattern categories. Words that do not fit the category could also be included (Schlagal & Schlagal, 1992).

Word bank bulletin board. To create a class reference tool for the emergent spelling classroom, use a bulletin board to post a word bank. Write the letters A to Z on library book pockets and put them on the bulletin board in alphabetical order. As words come up in the life of the classroom, the teacher or students can write the words on index cards and file them in the correct pocket. As children are writing, they may refer to the word bank for spelling needs or they may add interesting words of their own. This working bulletin board may then be used for strategy lessons on spelling, alphabetical order, phonics, word patterns and word sorts.

Word games. Games like Hangman, I Spy, and class versions of Scrabble® and Wheel of Fortune® can direct children's attention to words and their spellings within an atmosphere of play.

Personal dictionaries. Students may keep their own card file or word book to refer to when writing. Words they have learned to spell or words of particular interest to them may be included. An ongoing collection of words such as this can be helpful in noting spelling growth.

Irregular spellings. Since fostering independence is a spelling goal, teachers should not normally give students spellings. However, this can be very difficult when a child wants to use an irregularly spelled word. Holdaway (1979) suggests giving the student the irregular part of the word and asking her or him to complete the rest.

Word hunt. Bloodgood (1991) describes an activity where children are given a word such as pain and then they search their pieces of writing, books they are reading, labels and signs around the room, charts, etc. for words with the same spelling characteristics.

Discovering the rules. When a teacher notices an error being made by several members of a class, this word pattern may be put on the board to study. The teacher points out the pattern, and then the students add other words that fit the pattern. The spelling rule that governs the pattern is discovered and discussed. An example would be *-ing* words: *come/coming, bake/baking, write/writing*. The rule of dropping a silent *e* when adding a suffix would be reinforced (Routman, 1991).

Applying the known to the unknown. Reminding children of words they know how to spell can help them spell new words. If the children know how to spell the word *like*, the teacher can help them spell the word *spike*. As this strategy is used consistently in the classroom, it becomes part of the students' own repertoire of spelling strategies they can use to help themselves.

In spite of the promise of new strategies in spelling instruction, some children will not learn spelling easily because they are not able to master visual features of words. This aspect of spelling will always be a puzzle to educators (Graves, 1983). Graves cites work done in the 1930s and 1940s that showed spelling proficiency is unrelated to intelligence. The sad thing is that many poor spellers in our schools today feel unsuccessful and have little motivation for writing because of the overemphasis on correct spelling in the classroom. Poor spellers can be exceptional writers if we put spelling in its proper place (Graves, 1983).

Whether a child is a poor speller or one who learns words easily, we can provide a meaningful spelling program. As informed professionals we need to capitalize on strengths, encourage risk taking, and celebrate our students' progress.

REFERENCES

Adams, M. (1990). *Beginning to read: Thinking and learning about print, a summary*. Urbana-Champaign, IL: University of Illinois, Center for the Study of Reading.

Bartch, J. (1992). An alternative to spelling: An integrated approach. *Language Arts, 69,* 404–408.

Bean, W., & Bouffler, C. (1991). *Spell by writing*. Portsmouth, NH: Heinemann.

Bloodgood, J. (1991) A new approach to spelling instruction in language arts programs. *The Elementary School Journal, 92,* 203–211.

Buchanan, E. (1989). *Spelling for whole language classrooms*. Winnipeg, MB, Canada: Whole Language Consultants.

Butler, A., & Turbill, J. (1987). *Towards a reading-writing classroom*. Portsmouth, NH: Heinemann.

Calkins, L. (1986). *The art of teaching writing*. Portsmouth, NH: Heinemann.

Fehring, H., & Thomas, V. (1989). *The teaching of spelling*. Victoria, Australia: Ministry of Education.

Gentry, J. (1987). *Spel...is a four-letter word*. Portsmouth, NH: Heinemann.

Graves, D. (1983). *Writing: Teachers and children at work*. Portsmouth, NH: Heinemann.

Griffith, P. (1991). Phonemic awareness helps first graders invent spellings and third graders remember correct spellings. *Journal of Reading Behavior, 23,* 215–232.

Holdaway, D. (1979). *The foundations of literacy*. Gosford, NSW, Australia: Ashton Scholastic.

Routman, R. (1991). *Invitations: Changing as teachers and learners K–12*. Portsmouth, NH: Heinemann.

Schlagal, R., & Schlagal, J. (1992). The integral character of spelling: Teaching strategies for multiple purposes. *Language Arts, 69,* 418–424.

Wilde, S. (1990). A proposal for a new spelling curriculum. *The Elementary School Journal, 90,* 275–289.

Wilde, S. (1992). *You kan red this!* Portsmouth, NH: Heinemann.

An essential vocabulary: An update

Anita P. Davis
Thomas R. McDaniel

VOLUME 52, NUMBER 3, NOVEMBER 1998

Are there "essential words"—words so important for survival and success in everyday life that everyone should know them? Corlett T. Wilson thought so and published his recommendations in the November 1963 issue of *The Reading Teacher* . He did not attempt to include as many words as possible. Rather, Wilson sought to keep this necessary vocabulary at an absolute minimum and stressed the importance of teaching these essential phrases and words to everyone—especially the disabled reader. Table 1 gives Wilson's Essential Vocabulary.

Still with us today is the 1960s problem: too many people who cannot read the printed word—yet many printed words are essential to survival. Remedial readers, adults in literacy programs, and non–English-speaking people have not disappeared with time; they have, in fact, increased in some geographical areas. Visitors, pedestrians, drivers, and employees must still quickly recognize many complicated written words and phrases and must make immediate decisions to avoid hazardous situations, socially unacceptable behavior, and embarrassment. The disabled reader, the non–English-speaking person, and the young child do not always have the benefit of pictures, phonetic skills, a companion who can read, or adequate context clues to aid them in deciphering the messages in print; society continues to expect them to recognize many key words and phrases that appear on doors, on signs, and on labels.

With the passage of time and the development of a more complex society, the number of essential words has increased. The health hazards apparent 30 years ago pale in comparison to today's hazards. Hospital visitors now routinely receive printed warnings to avoid radiation areas, X-ray devices, biohazards, and smoking. Signs now caution pedestrians, warn that microwave ovens are in use in certain establishments, state that soliciting is prohibited, and alert that hard hats are required in construction areas. Ignoring these printed messages, and others, can

Table 1
The original essential vocabulary

adults only	first aid	nurse
antidote	flammable	office
beware	found	open
beware of the dog	fragile	out
bus station	gasoline	out of order
bus stop	gate	pedestrians prohibited
caution	gentlemen	poison
closed	handle with care	poisonous
combustible	hands off	police (station)
contaminated	help	post no bills
condemned	high voltage	post office
deep water	inflammable	posted
dentist	information	private
don't walk	instructions	private property
do not cross, use	keep away	pull
tunnel	keep closed at all times	push
do not crowd	keep off (the grass)	safety first
do not enter	keep out	shallow water
do not inhale	ladies	shelter
fumes	live wires	smoking prohibited
do not push	lost	step down (up)
do not refreeze	men	taxi stand
do not shove	next (window)	terms cash
do not stand up	(gate)	thin ice
do not use near	no admittance	this end up
heat	no checks cashed	this side up
do not use near	no credit	up
open flame	no diving	use before (date)
doctor (Dr.)	no dogs allowed	use in open air
down	no dumping	use other door
dynamite	no fires	violators will be
elevator	no fishing	prosecuted
emergency exit	no hunting	walk
employees only	no loitering	wanted
entrance	no minors	warning
exit	no smoking	watch your step
exit only	no spitting	wet paint
explosives	no swimming	women
external use only	no touching	
fallout shelter	no trespassing	
fire escape	not for internal use	
fire extinguisher	noxious	

Note: Words and phrases in this list were selected on the basis of their importance to physical safety, social acceptability, and the avoidance of embarrassment. This recommended list is for remedial reading and adult literacy programs at all educational levels.

Table 2
Updated list of essential words

10 items or less
30 days same as cash
911
airbags
alternate route
aluminum cans only
ambulance
asbestos hazard
automatic
biohazard
biohazardous waste
blasting zone
bomb threat
breakable
bridge ices before road
buckle up
bump
business route
by-pass
caffeine
cancerous
cash only
cellular phones prohibited
chemicals
children at play
clearance
construction ahead
consult physician
before use
danger
dangerous
deer crossing
delay
deliveries
detour
diesel fuel
directions
dispose
do not bend
do not block intersection
do not enter
do not get in eyes
do not ingest

do not mix
do not take if allergic to...
do not take with milk
do not use near water, fire,
   etc.
don't walk
dosage
drive in
drive through
drive up window
electrical hazard
Emergency Medical
   Services
enter only
escalator
exact change (needed
   or only)
exit only
expect delays
expiration
expires (EXP)
explosives
express line
evacuate
falling rock
fasten seat belt
fax machine
fire alarm
fire exit
flagger ahead
flush
for help dial *HP
form line here
handicapped parking
hard hat area
harmful
hazard
hazardous
hazardous area
hazardous chemicals
hazardous waste
help wanted
hospital

ID required
if swallowed, induce vomit-
   ing
in case of fire
incinerate
incinerator
infectious area
insert card (ATM)
irritant
keep away from water
keep frozen
keep out of reach of children
keep refrigerated
kerosene
lifeguard on duty
loading zone
makes wide turns
manager
may cause birth defects
may cause dizziness
may cause drowsiness
microwave in use
microwave safe
minimum speed
must be 21 years of age
no jet skis allowed
no left turn
no littering
no outlet
no pagers
no parking
no pets
no photographs permitted
no refunds
no returns
no through traffic
no turn on red
no video cameras allowed
non-alcoholic
non-toxic
nuclear waste
one way
order here

(continued)

Table 2
Updated list of essential words (continued)

oxygen in use	school crossing	tornado watch
pay cashier before pumping	school zone	tow away zone
pay here	service engine	tow zone
pedestrian crossing	self service	toxic
polluted area	shake well	toxic waste
prepare to stop	shirt and shoes required	turn off cellular phones
quiet please	signature	turn signal
radiation hazard	slippery when wet	uneven shoulder
radioactive materials	slow down	use only as directed
radioactive waste	soft shoulders	ventilation required
railroad crossing	speed limit	video camera in use
read directions before using	stairs (stairway)	video monitor in use
recyclable	stop ahead	watch for falling rocks
recycle	subway	watch for trucks
refrigerate	surgeon general warning	wear protective eye gear
restricted area	take with food	wear safety glasses
restrooms	teller machine	weight limit
resume safe speed	through traffic	wide load
right of way	time card	wrong way
right turn only	time clock	X-ray
road closed	tornado warning	yield

result in inconvenience, arrest, embarrassment, serious injury, or even death for the unaware individual.

Because the number of hazards, rules, and laws in a complex society has grown, the need for an updated list of survival or essential words has also increased. During 1996–1997 graduate and undergraduate students in a course in developmental reading decided to update Wilson's original list of essential words, words that teachers must often teach as sight words—even at a time when many instructors are downplaying the use of the whole-word method. Table 2 contains the additional words that teachers and future teachers considered to be most crucial.

The recognition of these key words and phrases may require non–English-speaking individuals, disabled readers, and adult literacy students—particularly those who cannot use phonic analysis or context clues effectively—to use rote memorization for mastery. Reading programs for adults and young people should ideally incorporate these necessary words. Teachers and future teachers should routinely consider the list carefully, use it appropriately, and update it as necessary to reflect changing needs and concerns of a dynamic society.

REFERENCE

Wilson, C.T. (1963). An essential vocabulary. *The Reading Teacher, 17*, 94–96.

Word Storm: Connecting vocabulary to the student's database

Ronald M. Klemp

VOLUME 48, NUMBER 3, NOVEMBER 1994

The Word Storm (see the Figure) is an activity that juxtaposes the use of vocabulary words in context with the students' speculation about their functional application. It may be used as a preteaching activity to familiarize students with more specialized vocabulary. Students work in pairs or small groups, and words are divided among the class so that no more than two groups will have the same word. Duplication of words provides further insights into uses of the words during the response portion of the activity.

Students are given a Word Storm sheet with a word in the top space. Their task is to respond to each of the prompts on the activity sheet in any order, although the teacher might direct students to extract a sentence from the text in which the word appears as their first step. The students then talk about the different features of the word and try to fit information about the word into each of the categories.

During the information search, students can utilize a dictionary, glossary, thesaurus, or their own knowledge. Some categories have a degree of ambiguity, which may allow students to report differently. For example, to the prompt "What are some different forms of the word?" some students may respond by listing different parts of speech. Other students may report synonyms, while still others may report different tense variations of the word.

In some of the categories students may not be able to respond, since the word may not fit into that prompt. It is important for students to understand that words possess different qualities and that not all words are consistent in their usage. In this sense, a nonanswer is also valuable.

The Word Storm activity provides a pathway into community building. When the activity is used in pairs, a situation is created where students are teaching each other the words. Also, because of the high degree of participation and dialogue, in-

Word storm

Student's name _____

To understand a word, it is sometimes better to know more than just the dictionary definition. A word map lets you write down different types of information to help you understand what a word means and the many ways in which the word can be used.

What is the word? _____

Write the sentence from the text in which the word is used (use the space below):

_____

What are some words that you think of when you hear this word?

_____

What are some different forms of the word?_____

_____

Name three people who would be most likely to use the word besides teachers:

1. _____ 2. _____ 3. _____

What are some other ways of saying the same thing? _____

_____

Make up a sentence using this word. Let your sentence tell what the word means. _____

_____

terest remains high throughout the activity. Students might work together on one day and then report their responses to the class on successive days. During the reporting, students record information that they feel is relevant. Moreover, the teacher can assess when the class is ready to move forward through the material that was the source of the vocabulary. The interactive instruction offered by the Word Storm enables students to add to their store of information as vocabulary is integrated with content.

Anticipating Antipasto in Antarctica?

Jeannine Perry Rajewski

Volume 47, Number 8, May 1994

One of the strategies I teach early readers to use when they come to a word they don't know is to look for smaller words that they do know within the large word—the *got* or *ten* in *gotten*, the *pen* in *pencil*, or the *art* in *start*. Attending to the structure of words is a valuable strategy, but like all reading strategies it must be taught and used in meaningful context.

In first and second grade, one of the books we use for reading groups is *Horrible Harry and the Ant Invasion*, one of a series of books by Suzy Kline about a second-grade class. This particular Horrible Harry book launches students into a motivating, exciting, and very meaningful word hunt that illustrates the use and method of finding little words in larger ones, expands vocabulary, encourages creativity, and even promotes dictionary exploration.

In *Horrible Harry and the Ant Invasion*, the second-grade students in Room 2B set up an ant farm. When one students realizes the word ant can be found in many words, a hunt for ant words begins. In the story, students make posters of ants, actively illustrating the meaning of their ant word. They tape the posters all over the school hallways for their "ant invasion."

Needless to say, we begin our own *ant* invasion by first listing the *ant* words from *Horrible Harry* and then brainstorming more. As the days go on, more and more words are added to the list. Then we brainstorm clever ways to illustrate these words with ant figures. Natural discussions of nouns, verbs, adjectives, and adverbs arise from this activity.

At this point, I bring out a wonderful book called *Antics* by Cathi Hepworth. This alphabet book depicts ant words for each letter of the alphabet with highly creative illustrations featuring ants representing the word in some way. For example, S*ant*a Claus is an ant dressed in a red suit and immig*rant*s depicts a family of European ants at Ellis Island. The class creates posters and the invasion begins.

My students really enjoy this activity while they learn and practice an essential reading strategy in the context of the literature they are reading. Students become much more aware of word composition and launch their own hunts for little words in bigger ones. Students learn dictionary skills while looking for words. This topic could easily be integrated into other curricular areas like science and social studies with a class ant farm or through a study of communities.

CHILDREN'S BOOKS CITED

Hepworth, C. (1992). *Antics*. New York: Putnam.

Kline, S. (1991). *Horrible Harry and the ant invasion*. New York: Puffin.

Fun with vocabulary

Janet Towell

VOLUME 51, NUMBER 4, DECEMBER 1997/JANUARY 1998

A word

A word is dead
When it is said,
Some say.
I say it just
Begins to live
That day.

Emily Dickinson

The following acrostic is used to introduce enjoyable and effective strategies and activities for vocabulary instruction with elementary students. (An annotated list accompanies each letter.)

V Vocabulary Self-Collection Strategy; Visual-Auditory-Kinesthetic-Tactile
O Onsets and rimes
C Color shock; clusters
A ABC books; anagrams
B Book boxes; visual configuration boxes; banks for words
U Unusual and unknown words (word attack strategies)
L List-Group-Label; Language Experience Approach
A Active involvement (music, drama, and finger spelling)
R Repetition; rhymes; riddles; roots
Y Yarns

V: Vocabulary Self-Collection Strategy (VSS); Visual-Auditory-Kinesthetic-Tactile (VAKT)

Vocabulary Self-Collection Strategy (Haggard, 1986): After locating a new word in their environment, students are asked to share (a) where they found the word, (b) the context, and (c) the importance of the word and why they selected it. It is fun for the class to guess the meaning of the word from the context before the definition is read by the student who selected the word.

Visual-Auditory-Kinesthetic-Tactile: The Fernald is a popular multisensory technique (Tierney, Readence, & Dishner, 1980). Students are asked to trace the target word with a finger while pronouncing each syllable until it can be written from memory (with eyes closed at first). Ghost writing, writing in the air, or writing on a child's back can be helpful for practicing this technique. Learning disabled students benefit from using VAKT.

O: Onsets and rimes

This technique for developing phonemic awareness can help beginning readers quickly and effectively learn many sight words using word patterns. (The onset is the part of the word before the vowel; the rime includes the vowel and the rest of the letters in the word.) *Oopples and Boo-noo-noos* by Hallie Yopp and Ruth Yopp (1996) is highly recommended as a resource for learning more about phonemic awareness and word play. The book includes appropriate literature, songs, and activities.

C: Color shock; clusters

Color shock (Vitale, 1982) is a technique that was originally designed for right-brained, learning disabled students to help them remember sight words. Right-brained children seem to have a special sensitivity for bright colors. During this strategy, children write their vocabulary, spelling words, or multiplication tables in color shock (each letter or number is written in a different color, beginning with the color green for go to designate the beginning of the word). This technique has improved directionality, visual discrimination, and sequential memory skills in many learning disabled students.

Clusters: For vocabulary instruction to be meaningful, words should be presented in semantic frameworks through categories or clusters (Marzano & Marzano, 1988). A cluster is a set of words that relate to a single concept. Clustering is the process of relating a target word to a set of synonyms or other associated words. Clustering enables students to understand the target word better and retain it for a longer period of time.

A: ABC books; anagrams

ABC books: Alphabet books have been used successfully for teaching vocabulary, even at the secondary level (Pope & Polette, 1989). Students can be motivated to discover words through illustrations on the basis of their prior knowledge or schemata instead of memorizing the words from a required list. Through the use of complex alphabet books such as *The Ultimate Alphabet* (Wilks, 1992) and *Animalia* (Base, 1987), students are encouraged to identify synonyms, antonyms, and parts of speech for their self-selected words. Students may also enjoy creating their own ABC books based on selected themes, topics, or units of study.

Anagrams are another fun and interesting way to learn vocabulary or spelling words. In *The Eleventh Hour* by Graeme Base (1989), readers use anagrams and additional clues to solve a very complicated mystery. This book is a great way to introduce anagrams, and it appeals to all ages. (The answers are sealed in the back of the book for novice sleuths.) Students may also have fun figuring out lists of words in which the letters are scrambled. They can be "Word Detectives."

B: Book boxes; boxes for visual configuration; banks for words

Book boxes: Teachers and students collect objects or "realia" for key words or concepts in the story, placing them in a box along with the book and any other related reading materials. This technique is especially helpful for second-language learners.

Boxes for visual configuration (Thatcher, 1984): This visual discrimination technique involves drawing around words to emphasize their length and shape. It helps emergent readers distinguish between frequently confused letters and words, such as those with *b*, *p*, or *d*. They learn to recognize shapes before distinguishing individual letters or words.

Word banks: Students should have personal word banks for storing and remembering their self-selected and teacher-selected words, such as spelling words. During the year, students watch their word banks grow. These words may come from daily journals or reading materials. Index boxes, curtain rings, or blank books that are alphabetized serve as efficient organizers. Some teachers may prefer word walls that list high-frequency words or words in specific categories.

U: Unusual and unknown words

Unusual words: Sniglets, a term originally coined by Rich Hall, are fun to study in the intermediate grades and beyond (Atkinson & Longman, 1985). In one study, high school students created and defined Sniglets with common affixes and bases, including multiple meaning and parts of speech. This activity was a welcome change from the monotony of the usual vocabulary drill. An example of a Sniglet is *baldage* = hair left in the drain after showering (Hall, 1985).

Unknown words: The following word attack strategy is recommended for students in the primary grades:

1. Beep it. Say "beep" for the unknown word and read to the end of the sentence. Think of a word that would make sense in that space. Use context clues.

2. Frame it. Put index fingers around the word to separate it from the rest of the sentence.

3. Begin it. Look at the beginning sound or sounds (letter or blend).

4. Split it. Divide the word into syllables and pronounce them.

5. Find it. Look the word up in the dictionary or ask someone as a last resort.

L: List-Group-Label; Language Experience Approach

List-Group-Label (Readence & Searfoss, 1980): This is a great strategy to use with the ABC book *Animalia* by Graeme Base (1987). Working in cooperative groups, students list as many words as possible that begin with a specific letter on a piece of chart paper. (*Animalia* works well for this activity because it comes with a wall frieze that matches the book. The wall frieze comes in many different sections.) Students are give a time period to complete their lists (e.g., 15 minutes). The older the students, the more words/pictures they will be able to recognize because of their prior knowledge and schemata. After the lists of words are made and counted, students sort and label the words according to different categories. This makes the words more meaningful and easier to remember.

The *Language Experience Approach* is based on the premise that written language is actually oral language in printed form (Tierney et al., 1980). Dictated stories, word banks, and creative writing are emphasized. Language experience is an effective way to teach sight words to beginning readers or to older remedial readers who have limited sight vocabularies. Repeated reading is encouraged. There is natural motivation because the stories are usually related to the students' interests. Students are able to read successfully, perhaps for the first time. Publishing their stories in book formats for the class library can be powerful for building vocabulary as well as self-esteem.

A: Active involvement

If vocabulary instruction is to be effective, the students must be actively involved (Carr & Wixson, 1986; Nagy, 1988; Ruddell, 1986). Physical involvement such as hands-on activities to accommodate their kinesthetic-tactile learning styles can be effective. Having students do nonverbal skits, acting out the meanings of words, is another possibility (Riddell, 1988).

Music can be a motivator for learning vocabulary words or developing phonemic awareness. The vocabulary of college students improved when they used their vocabulary words in song-writing exercises (Baechtold & Algiers, 1986). For increasing phonemic awareness, Hallie Yopp (Yopp & Yopp, 1996) recommends songs based on popular tunes such as "If You're Happy and You Know It," "Someone's in the Kitchen with Dinah," "Old McDonald," and "Twinkle, Twinkle, Little Star."

Finger spelling with the manual alphabet is another strategy that actively involves students during vocabulary instruction. In the past, finger spelling has been used only for names, places, and words for which there were no signs (Sullivan & Bourke, 1980). By using 26 hand shapes, all the letters of the alphabet can be made and written in the air. Finger spelling/sign language has proven to be beneficial for improving word identification and spelling skills in both hearing and hearing-impaired children (Andrews, 1988; Isaacson, 1987; Wilson & Hafer, 1990).

R: Repetition; rhymes; riddles; roots

To facilitate comprehension of text, *repetition* of vocabulary is necessary to ensure quick and easy access of words during the reading process (Nagy, 1988). Vocabulary acquisition through repetition can be accomplished through language experience, choral reading, Readers Theatre, tape-recorded books, patterned or predictable books, basals, and rhymes in poetry.

Riddles can be used to introduce new vocabulary words for stories in basal readers or trade books. Students will enjoy writing and guessing riddles much more than writing sentences and definitions. Riddles could be a component of thematic units in an integrated curriculum. For instance, *Tyrannosaurus Wrecks* (Sterne, 1979) contains 145 riddles about dinosaurs. For example, What did the dinosaur cattle baron say to the outlaw? "Get off my terror-tory." Reading a riddle from the chalkboard each day is another exciting way for students to learn many new sight words. They may also enjoy bringing their own riddles to class.

Roots: The study of Latin, Greek, and English root words and affixes can greatly increase a student's vocabulary. Morphemic analysis and the study of etymology or word origins are especially beneficial for students in the intermediate grades and junior high. Deriving word meanings from their roots can be challenging and rewarding. For instance, the root *tele* (far) is found in the following words: *telecast, teleconference, telegram, telegraph, telephone, telescope, telethon,* and *television* (Tompkins, 1997, p. 171). Students can expand their word knowledge further through the exploration of the remaining roots in the words. For example, the root *phon* (sound) in *tele-phone* is found in *earphone, microphone, phonics, phonograph, saxophone,* and *symphony.* The possibilities are endless. An added benefit of this word study is to encourage students to use the dictionary.

Y: Yarns

Creating yarns or tall tales is an imaginative way for students to learn new vocabulary and/or concepts. One procedure is to divide the class into cooperative groups of four or five students. Select five meaningful vocabulary words from their next story. Challenge them to see which group can create the wildest, most exaggerated story using the same five words. Then let them read the real story and compare!

Summary

Remember to make vocabulary instruction as much fun as possible. Motivation, active involvement, repetition, and relevance lead to independent word learning, the goal of vocabulary instruction. This list of suggested strategies and activities provides a good start for teaching your students the power of words.

REFERENCES

Andrews, J. (1988). Deaf children's acquisition of prereading skills using the reciprocal teaching procedure. *Exceptional Children, 54,* 349–355.

Atkinson, R., & Longman, D. (1985). Sniglets: Give a twist to teenage and adult vocabulary instruction. *Journal of Reading, 29,* 103–105.

Baechtold, S., & Algiers, A. (1986). Teaching college students vocabulary with rhyme, rhythm, and ritzy characters. *Journal of Reading, 30,* 248–253.

Carr, E., & Wixson, K. (1986). Guidelines for evaluating vocabulary instruction. *Journal of Reading, 29,* 588–595.

Haggard, M. (1986). The vocabulary self-collection strategy: Using student interest and world knowledge to enhance vocabulary growth. *Journal of Reading, 30,* 634–642.

Hall, R., & Friends. (1985). *More sniglets.* New York: Macmillan.

Isaacson, A. (1987). A fingerspelling approach to spelling. *Academic Therapy, 23,* 89–90.

Marzano, R., & Marzano, J. (1988). *A cluster approach to vocabulary instruction.* Newark, DE: International Reading Association.

Nagy, W. (1988). *Teaching vocabulary to improve reading comprehension.* Newark, DE: International Reading Association.

Pope, C.A., & Polette, K. (1989). Using ABC books for vocabulary development in the secondary school. *English Journal, 78,* 78–80.

Readence, J., & Searfoss, L. (1980). Teaching strategies for vocabulary development. *English Journal, 69,* 43–46.

Riddell, C.B. (1988). Towards a more active vocabulary. *English Journal, 77,* 50–51.

Ruddell, R. (1986). Vocabulary learning: A process model and criteria for evaluation instructional strategies. *Journal of Reading, 30,* 581–587.

Sullivan, M., & Bourke, L. (1980). *A show of hands.* New York: Harper & Row.

Thatcher, J. (1984). *Teaching reading to mentally handicapped children.* London: Croom Helm.

Tierney, R.J., Readence, J.E., & Dishner, E.K. (1980). *Reading strategies and practices: A guide for improving instruction.* Boston: Allyn & Bacon.

Tompkins, G. (1997). *Literacy for the 21st century.* Upper Saddle River, NJ: Simon & Schuster.

Vitale, B. (1982). *Unicorns are real.* Rolling Hills Estates, CA: Jalmar Press.

Wilson, R., & Hafer, J. (1990). *Come sign with us.* Washington, DC: Galludet.

Yopp, H., & Yopp, R. (1996). *Oopples and boo-noo-noos: Songs and activities for phonemic awareness.* New York: Harcourt Brace.

CHILDREN'S LITERATURE CITED

Base, G. (1987). *Animalia.* New York: Harry N. Abrams.

Base, G. (1989). *The eleventh hour.* New York: Harry N. Abrams.

Sterne, N. (1979). *Tyrannosaurus wrecks.* New York: Harper & Row.

Wilks, M. (1992). *The ultimate alphabet.* New York: Holt.

A scaffolding technique to develop sentence sense and vocabulary

Evelyn T. Cudd
Leslie L. Roberts

VOLUME 47, NUMBER 4, DECEMBER 1993/JANUARY 1994

Written language is far more complex than spoken language in terms of the organization, vocabulary, and sentence structure. Children who seldom listen to or read books are deprived of exposure to the complex syntax that is found in written language (Purcell-Gates, 1989). Without this exposure, children are at a disadvantage both in understanding writers' syntactic constructions and in being able to choose appropriate constructions with which to convey meaning in their own writing.

We observed that our poorer readers in Grades 1 through 3, and often even our average and good readers, were not automatically making the transfer from book language to their own writing. Their writing lacked the precise vocabulary and varied syntax that we encouraged and drew students' attention to during reading.

We felt part of the problem was that many of these children did not come from reading backgrounds. They were not read to at home and were not independent readers at school. However, we also felt that we needed a more direct approach to teaching sentence structure and vocabulary. We already knew that exercises from the English grammar book on subjects and predicates and complete sentences had no transfer value and took up valuable time. Looking up definitions in the dictionary and filling in blanks on a ditto did not ensure use of targeted vocabulary in student writing.

After experimenting with various sentence manipulation activities, we decided that sentence expanding was the most effective method of introducing and reinforcing complex sentence structures. Having students complete sentence stems containing specific syntactic structures and vocabulary allowed them to use the syntax and vocabulary successfully. In Figure 1, for example, the basal vocabulary words *toil* and *furious* were embedded in the subordinate clause *while Stephanie toiled furiously to repair the spaceship.* After a brief brainstorming session, students expanded the clause into a sentence

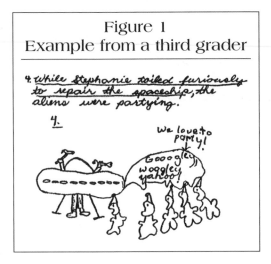

Figure 1
Example from a third grader

4. While stephanie toiled furiously to repair the spaceship, the aliens were partying.

4.

We love to party!

Gooogley woogley yahoo!

using their own ideas. Students then illustrated their sentences.

Procedures for using sentence expansion in the classroom

The following are procedures that we have developed to incorporate sentence expanding into our instructional program.

We begin by selecting vocabulary from the basal reader, trade books, or content area material to embed in the sentence stems. We do not hesitate to choose words from the highest level reading material in our classrooms. Because of the nature and structure of the activity, children of all ability levels can work successfully with challenging vocabulary. Next, we select a particular syntactic structure to introduce. This may be a structure that we have encountered during reading or simply one with which we want the chil-

dren to become more familiar. Then we embed the targeted vocabulary into sentence stems that, when expanded, will produce complex sentences (see Table for examples).

We personalize the sentence stems by adding children's names and familiar events, people, or places, drawing upon as much common experience as possible. Using children's names and common events helps to build class cohesion. Having each child as the subject of a sentence several times during the year is effective in building self-esteem.

When we have created two to five sentence stems, we write the sentences on the chalkboard or a chart. We go over each one briefly, discussing the concepts involved and eliciting ideas from students. As each student gives his or her response, we have the student repeat the complete sentence. This repetition provides oral reinforcement of the sentence structure and vocabulary after hearing it repeated in peer-generated sentences.

During these minilessons, students are guided through most of the steps of the writing process as they would be with longer compositions. As a part of the prewriting phase, attention is given not only to the sentence structure but to eliciting precise vocabulary and specific detail in student responses (see Figure 2). As students compose their sentences, they work with partners who are their peer editors.

After students have completed their writing and peer editing, we have them illustrate one or two sentences, encouraging them to add details to their drawings. It has been our experience that when chil-

Table
Example of clauses and phrases used as stems for sentence expansion

While on our daily journey to the cafeteria, _____

Behind the huge wooden door _____

Although Lauren is petite, _____

Ahead of the herd of stampeding elephants _____

After Rodney discovered the huge dinosaur bone, _____.

Before appearing on Hidden Oak News, _____

Besides collecting baseball cards, Tyrone _____

On top of the swaying flagpole _____

During Alberto's perilous journey across the Sahara Desert, _____

In addition to lifting weights, football players _____

As a result of the unexpected snowstorm,_____

Takeshia is so strong that_____

_____ is a teacher who _____

Note: Each stem is composed of vocabulary and syntactical structures the children have encountered in their basal reader, children's books, or content area material. Often the stem is a subordinate clause. As the primary school children (Grades 1–3) expand each stem. they produce complex sentences of the type that appear in written language—a step toward their own writing of complex prose.

Figure 2
Embedding similes and encouraging precise vocabulary and specific detail: Example from a first grader

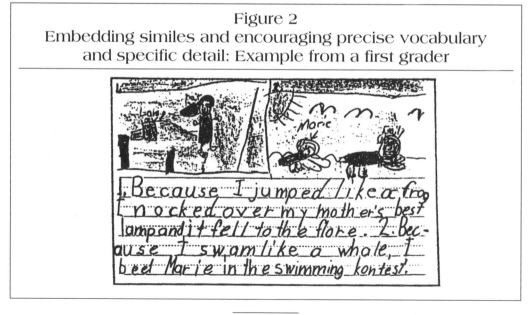

dren add details to their drawings to convey specific meaning, they are better able to understand the importance of adding details to convey a specific idea in writing. By recalling the details used in their illustrations, children have a concrete example of how details affect meaning.

We find that expansions of two to five sentences, with illustrations of one or two, produce the best results. We want to avoid the repetitious drill that has so often dominated independent practice in English grammar, reading, spelling, and vocabulary instruction.

Effects of structured practice

We have found the sentence expansion technique to be an effective and motivating way to teach sentence structure and vocabulary. We have observed an increased awareness of the importance of specific word choice and detail in our students' writing (see Figure 3).

Unedited beginning and midyear writing samples have revealed growth in vocabulary choice and sentence variety, even among our most disabled writers (see Figures 4 and 5).

According to Lawlor (1983), one way writers can gain better control over reading and writing is to make various elements of those processes routine in order to decrease the attention they require. Using sentence expansion, students learn to create complex sentences with sophisticated vocabulary in an encouraging and nonthreatening setting. As their under-

Figure 3
First paragraph of an original story written by a third grader

Thanksgiving Eve I was awakened by a soft but frightened gobble at my door. Quietly I crept to the window and peeked outside. There hovering under the bushes was the Terrified Turkey. Quick as a wink, I opened the door and in flapped Terry (Terry for short). Although he was exhausted, he gobbled out his problem.

Figure 4
Unedited writing samples from a disabled writer in third grade

Sample from first month of school

One day I had a horrible It was a real bad dad and this how it started. One dad I wokeup to eat bearkfast it was no creal and no eggs so I whent to the store and it was Som eggs and creal so I whent home and had my monning breakfast.

Sample 4 months later after practice in expanding sentences

When I was only eight years old I had to learn how to ride a Ten Speed and every day I fell off. Then one day I said Im going to quite and no one can make me do it again. I was mad that I would not talk. One day when there was no one home I gat my Ten Speed and I rode around the road and I was so glade that I still every body on my rode that I rode groud the rode. And I rode my bike every day.

Figure 5
Sentences written by a third-grade student who spoke nonstandard English—no stems provided

standing increases through practice, they gain better control over the writing process and begin to see themselves as writers. Incorporating their own ideas and personal experiences with guidance from their teachers, they gain confidence in their writing ability—confidence that could never be gained from copying textbook exercises or dictionary definitions.

REFERENCES

Lawlor, J. (1983). Sentence combining: A sequence for instruction. *The Elementary School Journal, 84,* 52–62.

Purcell-Gates, V. (1989). What oral/written language differences can tell us about beginning instruction. *The Reading Teacher, 42,* 290–294.

C(2)QU: Modeling context use in the classroom

Camille L.Z. Blachowicz

VOLUME 47, NUMBER 3, NOVEMBER 1993

Learning from context is a powerful means for building vocabulary, yet instructional ideas for modeling the contextual learning process are few and far between. Research suggests that teaching types and locations of context clues has limited impact (Stahl & Fairbanks, 1986). Instruction that focuses on the active problem solving processes involved in context use appears somewhat more promising (Baumann & Kameenui, 1991). Context instruction should involve students in the process of making hypotheses about meaning from what they already know or from their first look at a contextualized word and then cross-checking these hypotheses with other information (Blachowicz, 1987).

The process that is described below was formulated in several middle grade classrooms and was named C(2)QU (or SEE-TWO-CUE-YOU, in homage to *Star Wars!*) by students as a mnemonic for the steps in the process. As a mode of presenting new vocabulary, the purpose of C(2)QU is to present both definitional and contextual information about new words to students in a way that allows them to hypothesize about meaning, to articulate the cues that lead to the hypothesis, and to refine and use what they have learned with feedback from the group and from the teacher, if necessary. Classroom teachers developed the strategy, based on work about learning from context (Blachowicz & Zabroske, 1990; Gipe, 1979) and semantic manipulation of words for developing word meaning (Beck, Perfetti, & McKeown, 1982). The strategy has four steps:

C1: Give the word in a broad but meaningful *context*. For postreading vocabulary work this can be a usage selected from a story or chapter. Ask students to form hypotheses about the word's meaning; to give attributes, ideas or associations; and to "think aloud" to explain to the group the source of their hypotheses.

C2: Provide more explicit *context* with some definitional information. Ask students to reflect back on their initial ideas and to reaffirm or refine them again in a "think aloud" mode.

Q: Ask a *question* that involves semantic interpretation of the word. At this point you can also ask for a definition or give one if necessary. Discuss as needed with group members, using each other's cues and explanations as more data.

U: Ask students to *use* the word in meaningful sentences. Go back into the loop as needed.

Words suitable for the C(2)QU process are any that appear in reading material in a context that provides some information for hypothesizing. Most productive are new labels for already-known concepts or partially known words for which the context adds a new twist or further rich information. The process is not suitable for vocabulary that represents totally new concepts.

Instruction involves using a transparency on which the components can be revealed one at a time. For example, for the

---

Steps in C(2)QU for presenting new vocabulary

C1: [First example in context]
My new *stepmother* moved into our house after the wedding.
C2: [Second example in context]
When my father got married again, his new wife became my *stepmother*.
Q: [Question involving interpretation of the word]
Can a person have a mother and a stepmother at the same time?
U: [Teacher asks student to use word or give examples of attributes]

Note: Go back to the C(2)QU loop as needed for teaching each vocabulary item.

---

trade book *No One Is Going to Nashville* (Jukes, 1983), the teacher prepared the following transparency:

She revealed one line at a time and engaged students in the following dialogue:

T: [Reveals C1.] Will you read this sentence for me? (Students read.) What could *stepmother* mean?

S1: Like a second mother.

S2: Like when an orphan goes to another home.

T: [Reveals C2.] OK, look at this one. Does this match up with what we thought at first.

S1: Well, yeah. Like a second mother.

S3: More like if your mother dies or something, your dad can get another mother.

S2: Yea, in your home, not a foster home.

T: [Reveals Q.] Well, how about this. Could you have a mother and stepmother at the same time?

S4: No, there would only be one in your house.

S2: She didn't say they'd be in the same house. The question says can you have them at the same time. I have a mother and a stepmother. I live with my mother, but my stepmother lives with my dad.

(Further discussion, bringing in Cinderella, ensues.)

The teacher ended the session by asking students to use the word *stepmother* in their written summaries of the book, although she might have asked them to use it orally in a few examples if she had felt this was necessary.

With more confusing terms, such as homophones, teachers might structure the cross-checking that must take place in different ways. For a session on *The Heroine of Kapiti* (Dusault, 1974), a student gave the usage sentence, "I mist my bus." The teacher then went back to the two sample sentences:

The Maoris saw the snowy mountain peaks rise from the ocean mist.

Walking through the mist made my clothes all soggy and damp.

She asked the student for synonyms for *mist* in the samples and her own sentence. The student understood that "damp fog" and "didn't catch" were not equivalent and that "damp fog" was the more suitable interpretation.

For a difficult word like *verbatim*, the teacher might have students choose a correct usage from two alternatives before composing their own sentences:

She gave the message verbatim, using exactly the same words as her mother.

In a verbatim message, you can be creative and use your own language.

If students need more help, glossaries and dictionaries can be used, not to provide a formal definition but to help students cross-check information and construct their own definitions.

C(2)QU also provides an excellent model for cooperative reading groups. Research on word learning in cooperative groups suggests that students engage in little discussion or cross-checking when presenting new words and working in such groups unless they are first offered some

models as options (Fisher, Blachowicz, & Smith, 1991).

Teachers can first use C(2)QU, as above, in a larger group to model the process. Then the teacher can give selected students the job of "vocabulary director" and help them prepare materials for the words they wish to present for each chapter of their books. Students enjoy collaborating on the selection of words and the construction of sentences and questions. After the process has become familiar, vocabulary directors can set up all the C(2)QU materials, and the teacher can observe what takes place in the various groups. Besides allowing students to become responsible for their own learning, C(2)QU is fun for students to plan and execute and makes the vocabulary director's role a popular one.

C(2)QU helps students develop a context use process that involves rich discussion and monitoring their own learning. Besides being adaptable for whole-class or group use, it's enjoyable. Give it a try!

References

Baumann, J.F., & Kameenui, E.J. (1991). Research on vocabulary instruction: Ode to Voltaire. In J.F. Flood, J.M. Jensen, D. Lapp, & J. Squire (Eds.), *Handbook of research on teaching the English language arts* (pp. 603–632). New York: Macmillan.

Beck, I., Perfetti, C., & McKeown, M. (1982). Effects of long-term vocabulary instruction on lexical access and reading comprehension. *Journal of Educational Psychology, 74,* 506–521.

Blachowicz, C.L.Z., & Zabroske, B. (1990). Context instruction: A metacognitive approach for at-risk readers. *Journal of Reading, 33,* 504–508.

Blachowicz, J.A. (1987). Discovery as correction. *Synthese, 71,* 235–321.

Dusault, J. (1974). *The heroine of Kapiti.* London: Dorling-Kinderslee.

Fisher, P.J.L., Blachowicz, C.L.Z., & Smith, J.C. (1991). Vocabulary learning in literature discussion groups. In J. Zutell & S. McCormick (Eds.), *Learner factors/teacher factors: Issues in literacy research and instruction. Fortieth yearbook of the National Reading Conference* (pp. 201–209). Chicago: National Reading Conference.

Gipe, J. (1979). Investigating techniques for teaching new word meanings. *Reading Research Quarterly, 14,* 624–644.

Jukes, M. (1983). *No one is going to Nashville.* New York: Knopf.

Stahl, S.A., & Fairbanks, M.M. (1986). The effects of vocabulary instruction: A model-based meta-analysis. *Review of Educational Research, 56,* 72–110.

What's literacy?

Melissa Kotrla

VOLUME 50, NUMBER 8, MAY 1997

As a third-grade teacher, I learn everyday what I cannot take for granted. Though we had talked about environmental print (such as road signs and cereal boxes), I was surprised when I realized my students saw reading and writing unrelated to their world outside of school. I thought they would naturally make that leap between their own budding literacy at school and the literacy they encountered away from school.

I devised the following activity to help young students see the power of being literate and the profusion of literacy activities in the nonschool world. We did the activity as a prelude to International Literacy Day, but the activity can be done at any time of the year in celebration of literacy and the joy of being literate.

Our lesson started by analyzing the word *literacy* using a strategy called classical invention, based on Aristotle's principles in *Art of Rhetoric* (Carroll & Wilson, 1993). Classical invention helped the students understand the word by using the definition to find the relationship of the word to other parts of their world. Using thought prompts (see Figure), the students analyzed the word *literacy* in groups.

They recorded their ideas and findings on posters using drawings, quotes, and magazine pictures. Each group presented its poster to the class the following day. This created a base of knowledge about literacy for the students and gave them a context for the next activity (Carroll & Wilson, 1993).

Next, we took about a week to do a literacy scavenger hunt. The students discussed what kind of data to record in the hunt and drew up a chart. They set out to find as many examples of literacy as possible. Searching their school, homes, daycare facilities, and churches, they learned how to be people watchers. The students interviewed parents, grandparents, and neighbors to identify how reading and writing affects their duties at home and work.

At the end of the week we shared our findings. Students reported examples of every type of literacy from writing telephone messages on scraps of paper to reading formal work reports. It surprised several students to find that parents used reading and writing at work. For instance, one parent, a cashier, had to complete a report each evening. The children did not

Chart for groups to analyze literacy		
Classical invention principle	Group size	Thought prompts for group discussion
Definition	Whole class	Use several types of dictionaries to find a working definition of the word literacy.
Comparison	Small group 1	Use the definition to brainstorm topics that are the same as and different from literacy.
Relationship	Small group 2	What causes literacy? What effect does literacy have on people?
Circumstance	Small group 3	Who uses literacy? When do you see literacy? How is literacy a part of your life?
Testimony	Small group 4	What have you heard people say about literacy? Who have you heard talk about literacy? What do your classmates think about literacy?

realize that a cashier used writing. The children of computer programmers found that their parents not only used writing, but also had to understand and use a computer language. Several parents had to read and understand reports and memos. Seeing people in their families making grocery lists, reading newspapers, leaving notes for babysitters, studying for college courses, and reading recipes gave the students a rich context for reading and writing.

To analyze our findings, we used a categorizing technique called the affinity diagram (Cleary & Langford, 1995). Students wrote their literacy examples on sticky notes, one example on each piece of paper. They affixed their sticky notes to the chalkboard in categories according to similarity. This was done one or two students at a time, which gave them a chance to examine the developing categories and decide where to place their literacy examples. When an example did not fit an existing

category, a new category was made. The children also moved literacy examples to form subcategories like "reading for instructions" and "writing notes and letters." They were naturally drawn to thinking critically as they negotiated categories.

When all the examples were in place, the students labeled each category. We talked about how the categories had taken shape and how they could have been grouped differently. Looking back at the prompts we used to make the posters at the beginning of the week, we discussed where new knowledge from our hunt could be added. The students came to the conclusion that literacy was all around us and necessary for success.

To share our findings with others, the students illustrated one of their literacy examples. They used drawings, cartoon bubbles, and captions to create these literacy pictures. These, along with the posters, became our classroom decorations for a literacy celebration.

As a culminating activity, my literacy experts planned their literacy celebration using some of the same skills they saw others use. Jotting and listing as their party plans developed, the children grew more excited. Student-designed invitations welcomed parents and guest readers to a day that included reading with flashlights, singing songs, reading poems, and reading a recipe to make a snack.

During these activities, the students gained applicable knowledge of literacy, relating what we learned at school to what was happening away from school. The word *literacy* became a regularly used word in the classroom. Students came to class sharing more literacy discoveries all year. It gave them a natural context for our activities and lessons throughout the year and a jumping-off point for connections to other subjects.

In leading my students through these activities, I found something else I cannot take for granted: A context and a reason for learning give meaning to the student. I am learning to remember this.

REFERENCES

Carroll, J.A., & Wilson, E.E. (1993). *Acts of teaching: How to teach writing*. Englewood, CO: Teacher Ideas Press.

Cleary, B.A., & Langford, D.P. (1995). *Orchestrating learning with quality*. Milwaukee, WI: ASQC Quality Press.

The role of phonics in reading instruction

A position statement of the International Reading Association

The best approaches for how to teach children to read and write have been debated throughout much of the 20th century. Today, the role of phonics in reading and writing has become as much a political issue as it has an educational one. Teachers and schools have become the focus of unprecedented public scrutiny as the controversy over phonics is played out in the media, state legislatures, school districts, and the home. In response to the many requests that have been received, the International Reading Association offers the following position statement regarding the role of phonics in a total reading program.

We begin with three assertions regarding phonics and the teaching of reading. We conclude with an expression of concerns for the current state of affairs and a call for professionalism.

1. The teaching of phonics is an important aspect of beginning reading instruction.

This assertion represents a longstanding and widely shared view within the reading education community. The following statements from leaders in the field reveal the strength and history of this understanding.

"When the child has reached the maturity level at which he can make the best use of formal instruction in phonics, certainly no time should be lost in launching an extensive and carefully organized program to promote the wide and independent use of phonics in attacking new words, regardless of the grade or the time in the school year when this occurs."

Nila Banton Smith
IRA Founding Member

"Phonics instruction serves one purpose: to help readers figure out as quickly as possible the pronunciation of unknown words."

Dolores Durkin
Reading Hall of Fame Member

"Perhaps the most widely respected value of letter-sound instruction is that it provides students with a means of deciphering written words that are visually unfamiliar."

Marilyn Jager Adams
Author, *Beginning to Read: Thinking and Learning About Print*

"Phonics is a tool needed by all readers and writers of alphabetically written languages such as English. While I am not a proponent of isolated drill, overreliance on worksheets, or rote memorization of phonic rules, I support the teaching of phonics that children actually need and use to identify words quickly and accurately. These strategies need to be taught systematically in well-planned lessons."

Richard T. Vacca
IRA President, 1996–1997

"Early, systematic, explicit phonics instruction is an essential part, but only part, of a balanced, comprehensive reading program. Phonics and other word-identification skills are tools that children need to read for information, for enjoyment, and for developing insights. The intensity and form of phonics instruction must be adjusted to the individual needs of children by a well-prepared teacher."

John J. Pikulski
IRA President 1997–1998

We do not wish to suggest through these quotations that there is perfect harmony within the field regarding how phonics should be taught in a total reading program, rather that there is nearly unanimous regard for its importance.

2. Classroom teachers in the primary grades do value and do teach phonics as part of their reading programs.

A recent national study (Baumann, Hoffman, Moon, & Duffy, 1996) of reading instruction in American public schools found that 98% of primary-grade teachers regard phonics instruction as a very important part of their reading program. Further, the study found that primary-grade teachers engage their students in phonics lessons on a regular basis as part of instruction in reading and writing.

Although there are many different types of or approaches to phonics instruction (e.g., intensive, explicit, synthetic, analytic, embedded), all phonics instruction focuses the learner's attention on the relationships between sounds and symbols as an important strategy for word recognition. Teaching phonics, like all teaching, involves making decisions about what is best for children. Rather than engage in debates about whether phonics should or should not be taught, effective teachers of reading and writing ask when, how, how much, and under what circumstances phonics should be taught. Programs that constrain teachers from using their professional judgment in making instructional decisions about what is best in phonics instruction for students simply get in the way of good teaching practices.

3. Phonics instruction, to be effective in promoting independence in reading, must be embedded in the context of a total reading/language arts program.

Reading is the complex process of understanding written texts. Children learn to read by using many sources of information such as their experiences, illustrations and print on the page, and knowledge of language—including their knowledge of sound-symbol correspondences. When teachers share interesting and informative books, nursery rhymes, songs, and poems with predictable language patterns, children develop and refine their use of these various information sources. Children become aware of and understand how print on a page relates to meaning. When children engage with texts themselves, as readers or writers, they begin to orchestrate this knowledge of how written language works to achieve success. It is within these kinds of contexts of language use that direct instruction in phonics takes on meaning for the learner. When phonics instruction is linked to children's genuine efforts to read and write, they are motivated to learn. When phonics instruction is linked to children's reading and writing, they are more likely to become strategic and independent in their use of phonics than when phonics instruction is drilled and practiced in isolation. Phonics knowledge is critical but not sufficient to support growing independence in reading.

A Professional Stance Toward Phonics

The International Reading Association supports:

- research into effective phonics instruction and how this instruction supports the development of reading and writing abilities;
- teacher education initiatives at the preservice and inservice levels that encourage broader use of best practices in the teaching of phonics;

- parent education that is informative regarding the place of phonics within the total view of reading development and what parents can do to be supportive;
- curriculum development that helps articulate the specific goals of phonics instruction within the context of a total reading program, as well as suggestions for tools and strategies for effective teaching; and,
- authors and other artists who create the kind of engaging literature that provides the rich linguistic context for effective reading instruction.

The International Reading Association is concerned with:

- the exaggerated claims found in the press and other media regarding the inattention to phonics in beginning reading instruction;
- the growth in the number of curricular and legislative mandates that require teachers to blindly follow highly prescriptive plans for phonics instruction;
- the distortions in the professional literature surrounding the place of phonics instruction in a well-rounded, comprehensive reading program;
- the pitting of phonics against literature, as if the two are incompatible or at odds with each other; and,
- the inaccurate claims in the public media regarding the failure rates of students in learning to read that are attributed to the lack of phonics instruction.

Teachers *are* being successful in helping children learn to read. Every U.S. study of reading achievement conducted over the past two decades has reported increasing numbers of primary-grade students performing successfully. A recent international comparison study (Binkley & Williams, 1996) has shown that in the area of reading, primary-aged students from the United States outperformed students from all other countries but one. Recognition for the tremendous advances that have been made by teachers in the teaching of reading is long overdue. We applaud teachers for the great strides they have made in improving the quality of reading instruction for all students.

We are not satisfied with the achievement levels reflected in the national assessments or the international comparisons. We will not be satisfied until we can claim success for all children. We have a long way to go and there is much to learn. However, exaggerated claims of the failure of students in learning to read serve only to divert our attention, energies, and resources from the important issues we must face. Explanations that focus on simple solutions like more phonics instruction are misguided. The problems we face are complex and require inquiring minds.

Toward this end, the International Reading Association will continue to promote research and professional development activities focused on literacy. Through our research we will continue to study more effective ways of teaching reading, including phonics instruction, to achieve our common goal of literacy for all.

REFERENCES

Adams, M.J. (1990). *Beginning to read: Thinking and learning about print.* Cambridge, MA: MIT Press.

Baumann, J., Hoffman, J., Moon, J., & Duffy, A. (1996, December). *The first "R" in 21st Century Classrooms.* Paper presented at the Annual Meeting of the National Reading Conference, Charleston, SC.

Binkley, M., & Williams, T. (1996). *Reading literacy in the United States: Findings from the IEA reading literacy study* (Report No. NCES 96-258). Washington, DC: U.S. Department of Education Office of Educational Research and Improvement.

Durkin, D. (1989). *Teaching them to read.* Needham Heights, MA: Allyn & Bacon, 218.

Pikulski, J.J. (1997, January). *Becoming a nation of readers: Pursuing the dream.* Paper presented at the meeting of the Wisconsin State Reading Association, Milwaukee, WI.

Smith, N.B. (1963). *Reading instruction for today's children.* Englewood Cliffs, NJ: Prentice-Hall, 213.

Vacca, R.T. (1996, October/November). The reading wars: Who will be the winners, who will be the losers? *Reading Today, 14,* p. 3.

Single copies of International Reading Association position statements are available in PDF format through the IRA Web site (www.reading.org/advocacy/policies). Or, send a self-addressed, stamped No. 10 envelope to International Reading Association, Attn. Dept. E.G., 800 Barksdale Road, PO Box 8139, Newark, DE 19714-8139, USA. To purchase multiple copies, visit the Association's Online Bookstore: bookstore.reading.org.

Phonemic awareness and the teaching of reading

A position statement from the Board of Directors of the International Reading Association

Much has been written regarding phonemic awareness, phonics, and the failure of schools to teach the basic skills of reading. The Board of Directors offers this position paper in the hope of clarifying some of these issues as they relate to research, policy, and practice.

We view research and theory as a resource for educators to make informed instructional decisions. We must use research wisely and be mindful of its limitations and its potential to inform instruction.

What is phonemic awareness?

There is no single definition of phonemic awareness. The term has gained popularity in the 1990s as researchers have attempted to study early literacy development and reading disability. Phonemic awareness is typically described as an insight about oral language and in particular about the segmentation of sounds that are used in speech communication. Phonemic awareness is characterized in terms of the facility of the language learner to manipulate the sounds of oral speech. A child who possesses phonemic awareness can segment sounds in words (for example, pronounce just the first sound heard in the word *top*) and blend strings of isolated sounds together to form recognizable word forms. Often, the term *phonemic awareness* is used interchangeably with the term *phonological awareness*. To be precise, phonemic awareness refers to an understanding about the smallest units of sound that make up the speech stream: phonemes. Phonological awareness encompasses larger units of sound as well, such as syllables, onsets, and rimes. We use the term phonemic awareness in this document because much of the theoretical and empirical literature focuses specifically on phonemes. We also choose to use this term because of its more common use in the professional literature and in professional discussions.

Why the sudden interest in phonemic awareness?

The findings regarding phonemic awareness are not as new to the field of literacy as some may think, although it is only in recent years that they have gained wide attention. For over 50 years discussions have continued regarding the relation between a child's awareness of the sounds of spoken words and his or her ability to read. In the 1940s some psychologists noted that children with reading disabilities were unable to differentiate the spoken word into its sounds and put together the sounds of a word. Psychological research intensified during the 1960s and 1970s. Within the reading educational community there was research (for example, the "First-Grade Studies" in 1967) hinting at the important relation between sound awareness and learning to read.

Recent longitudinal studies of reading acquisition have demonstrated that the acquisition of phonemic awareness is highly predictive of success in learning to read—in particular in predicting success in learning to decode. In fact, phonemic awareness abilities in kindergarten (or in that age range) appear to be the best single predictor of successful reading acquisition. There is converging research evidence to document this relation, and few scholars would dispute this finding. However, there is considerable disagreement about what the relation means in terms of understanding reading acquisition and what the relation implies for reading instruction.

Isn't phonemic awareness just a 1990s word for phonics?

Phonemic awareness is not phonics. Phonemic awareness is an understanding about spoken language. Children who are phonemically aware can tell the teacher that *bat* is the word the teacher is representing by saying the three separate sounds in the word. They can tell you all the sounds in the spoken word *dog*. They can tell you that, if you take the last sound off *cart*, you would have *car*. Phonics, on the other hand, is knowing the relation between specific, printed letters (including combinations of letters) and specific, spoken sounds. You are asking children to show their phonics knowledge when you ask them which letter makes the first sound in *bat* or *dog* or the last sound in *car* or *cart*. The phonemic awareness tasks that have predicted successful reading are tasks that demand that children attend to spoken language, not tasks that simply ask students to name letters or tell which letters make which sounds. In fact, if phonemic awareness just meant knowledge of letter-sound relations, there would have been no need to coin a new term for it.

How does phonemic awareness work to facilitate reading acquisition?

That phonemic awareness predicts reading success is a fact. We can only speculate on why the strong relation exists. One likely explanation is that phonemic awareness supports understanding of the alphabetic principle—an insight that is crucial in reading an alphabetic orthography. The logic of alphabetic print is apparent to learners if they know that speech is made up of a sequence of sounds (that is, if they are phonemically aware). In learning to read, they discover that it is those units of sound that are represented by the symbols on a page. Printed symbols may appear arbitrary to learners who lack phonemic awareness.

If phonemic awareness is the best predictor of success in beginning reading, shouldn't we put all our time and effort in kindergarten and early reading into developing it?

Most researchers in this area advocate that we consciously and purposefully attend to the development of phonemic awareness as a part of a broad instructional program in reading and writing. Certainly, kindergarten children should have many opportunities to engage in activities that teach them about rhyme, beginning sounds, and syllables. How much time is needed for this kind of focused instruction is something only the teacher can determine based on a good understanding of the research on phonemic awareness and of his or her students' needs and abilities. Research suggests that different children may need different amounts and forms of phonemic awareness instruction and experiences. The research findings related to phonemic awareness suggest that although it might be necessary, it is certainly not sufficient for producing good readers. One thing is certain: We cannot give so much attention to phonemic-awareness instruction that other important aspects of a balanced literacy curriculum are left out or abandoned.

Is phonemic awareness a single, momentary insight? Or, is it best described as a skill that develops gradually over time?

Phonemic awareness has been measured using a variety of tasks that appear to tap into an individual's ability to manipulate the sounds of oral language. However, some tasks may require a more sophisticated understanding of sound structures than others. For example, rhyming appears much earlier than segmentation abilities for most children. Also, it seems to matter that children can hear the sounds of a spoken word in order, but it is not clear how early or late this ability does or should develop. Researchers are still working to identify the kinds of tasks and what aspects of phonemic awareness they might tap. It appears from the research that the acquisition of phonemic awareness occurs over time and develops gradually into more and more sophisticated levels of control. Some research suggests that there is a diversity of developmental paths among children. How much control is necessary for the child to discover the alphabetic principle is still unclear. There is no research evidence to suggest that there is any exact sequence of acquisition of specific sounds in the development of phonemic awareness, only that there is increasing control over sounds in general.

It has been stressed that phonemic awareness is an oral language skill and that it has nothing to do with print, letters, or phonics. Is this true?

It is true that phonemic awareness is an insight about oral language, and that you can assess phonemic awareness through tasks that offer no reference to print. However, to suggest that there is no relation between the development of phonemic awareness and print is misleading. There is evidence to suggest that the relation between phonemic awareness and learning to read is reciprocal: phonemic awareness supports reading acquisition, and reading instruction and experiences with print facilitate phonemic awareness development. The question remains as to the amount and forms of phonemic awareness one must have in order to profit from reading instruction that is focused on decoding. For instance, some research suggests that the abilities to blend and isolate sounds in the speech stream support reading acquisition while the ability to delete sounds from spoken words is a consequence of learning to read. The precise relation between phonemic awareness abilities and reading acquisition remains under investigation.

How can phonemic awareness be taught?

The answer to this question has both theoretical and practical implications. Theorists interested in determining the causal contribution of phonemic awareness to learning to read have conducted experimental studies in which some students are explicitly taught phonemic awareness and some are not. Many of the early studies in this genre focused on treatments that emphasize oral language work only. The findings from these studies suggest phonemic awareness can be taught successfully.

More recently, there have been studies of phonemic awareness training that combine and contrast purely oral language approaches to the nurturing of phonemic awareness abilities, with approaches that include interaction with print during the training. These studies suggest that programs that encourage high levels of student engagement and interaction with print (for example, through read-alouds, shared reading, and invented spelling) yield as much growth in phonemic awareness abilities as programs that offer only a focus on oral language teaching. These studies also suggest that the greatest impact on phonemic awareness is achieved when there is both interaction with print and explicit attention to phonemic awareness abilities. In other words, interaction with print combined with explicit attention to sound structure in spoken words is the best vehicle toward growth.

Some research suggests that student engagement in writing activities that encourage invented spelling of words can promote the development of phonemic awareness. These findings also are consistent with continuing research into the sources of influence on phonemic awareness abilities before students enter school. It is clear that high levels of phonemic awareness among very young children are related to home experiences that are filled with interactions with print (such as being read to at home, playing letter games and language play, and having early writing experiences).

Do all children eventually develop phonemic awareness? Shouldn't we just let them develop this understanding naturally?

Naturally is a word that causes many people difficulty in describing language development and literacy acquisition. In so far as it is natural for parents to read to their children and engage them with print and language, then phonemic awareness may develop naturally in some children. But if we accept that these kinds of interactions are not the norm, then we have a great deal of work to do in encouraging parents to engage their young children with print. We need to provide the information, the tools, and the strategies that will help them ensure that their young children will be successful in learning to read.

In schooling, the same advice holds true. Most children—estimated at more than 80%—develop phonemic awareness by the middle of first grade. Is this natural? Yes, if the natural model of classroom life includes opportunities to engage with print in a variety of ways and to explore language. However, we know that there are many classrooms where such engagement and explicit attention to sounds and print are not natural. We must equip teachers with the information, tools, and strategies they need to provide these kinds of learning opportunities in their classrooms.

The problem is most severe in terms of consequences when the students from economically disadvantaged homes, where the resources and parent education levels are lowest, enter schools that have limited resources and experience in promoting engagement with print. The students who need the most attention may be those who receive the least. We have a responsibility in these situations to not rely on the "natural" and to promote action that is direct, explicit, and meaningful.

What does this mean for classroom practice?

First, it is critical that teachers are familiar with the concept of phonemic awareness and that they know that there is a body of evidence pointing to a significant relation between phonemic awareness and reading acquisition. This cannot be ignored.

Many researchers suggest that the logical translation of the research to practice is for teachers of young children to provide an environment that encourages play with spoken language as part of the broader literacy program. Nursery rhymes, riddles, songs, poems, and read-aloud books that manipulate sounds may be used purposefully to draw young learners' attention to the sounds of spoken language. Guessing games and riddles in which sounds are manipulated may help children become more sensitive to the sound structure of their language. Many activities already used by preschool and primary-grade teachers can be drawn from and will become particularly effective if teachers bring to them an understanding about the role these activities can play in stimulating phonemic awareness.

What about the 20% of children who have not achieved phonemic awareness by the middle of first grade?

The research on this statistic is as clear as it is alarming. The likelihood of these students becoming successful readers is slim under current instructional plans.

We feel we can reduce this 20% figure by more systematic instruction and engagement with language early in students' home, preschool, and kindergarten classes.

We feel we can reduce this figure even further through early identification of students who are outside the norms of progress in phonemic awareness development, and through the offering of intensive programs of instruction.

Finally, there may be a small percentage of the students who may have some underlying disability that inhibits the development of phonemic awareness. Several scholars speculate that this disability may be at the root of dyslexia. More research is needed in this area, however. There is some promise here in the sense that we may have located a causal factor toward which remedial assistance can be tailored.

Some people advocate that primary teachers allocate large amounts of time to teaching students how to perform better on phonemic awareness tasks. There are no longitudinal studies that support the effectiveness of this practice in increasing the reading achievement of the children when they reach the intermediate grades.

What position does the International Reading Association take regarding phonemic awareness and the teaching of reading?

The International Reading Association already has issued a position paper on the role of phonics in the teaching of reading. That paper stresses the importance of phonics in a comprehensive reading program.

In this position statement we have attempted to elaborate on the complex relation between phonemic awareness and reading. We do so without taking away from our commitment to balance in a comprehensive reading program.

On the positive side, research on phonemic awareness has caused us to reconceptualize some of our notions about reading development. Certainly, this research is helping us understand some of the underlying factors that are associated with some forms of reading disability. Through the research on phonemic awareness we now have a clearer theoretical framework for understanding why some of the things we have been doing all along support development (for example, work with invented spelling). Additionally, the research has led us to new ideas that we should continue to study.

On the negative side, we are concerned that the research findings about phonemic awareness might be misused or overgeneralized. We are very concerned with policy initiatives that require teachers to dedicate specific amounts of time to phonemic awareness instruction for all students, or to policy initiatives that require the use of particular training programs for all students. Such initiatives interfere with the important instructional decisions that professional teachers must make regarding the needs of their students. We feel the following suggestions for good reading instruction will lead to the development of phonemic awareness and success in learning to read:

- Offer students a print-rich environment within which to interact;

- Engage students with surrounding print as both readers and writers;

- Engage children in language activities that focus on both the form and the content of spoken and written language;

- Provide explicit explanations in support of students' discovery of the alphabetic principle; and

- Provide opportunities for students to practice reading and writing for real reasons in a variety of contexts to promote fluency and independence.

We must keep in mind, though, that it is success in learning to read that is our goal. For students who require special assistance in developing phonemic awareness, we should be prepared to offer the best possible instruction and support.

SUGGESTED READINGS

1. What is phonemic awareness?

Adams, M.J. (1990). *Beginning to read: Thinking and learning about print*. Cambridge, MA: Massachusetts Institute of Technology Press.

Calfee, R.C., & Norman, K.A. (in press). *Psychological perspectives on the early reading wars: The case of phonological awareness*. Teachers College Record.

Share, D.L. (1995). Phonological recoding and self-teaching: Sine qua non of reading acquisition. *Cognition, 55*, 151–218.

Stahl, S.A., & Murray, B. (1998). Issues involved in defining phonological awareness and its relation to early reading. In J.L. Metsala &

L.C. Ehri (Eds.), *Word recognition in beginning literacy*. Hillsdale, NJ: Erlbaum.

Yopp, H.K. (1988). The validity and reliability of phonemic awareness tests. *Reading Research Quarterly, 23*, 159–177.

2. Why the sudden interest in phonemic awareness?

Bradley, L., & Bryant, P.E. (1983). Categorizing sounds and learning to read: A causal connection. *Nature, 301*, 419–421.

Goswami, U., & Bryant, P. (1990). *Phonological skills and learning to read*. Hove, UK: Erlbaum.

MacDonald, G.W., & Cornwall, A. (1995). The relationship between phonological awareness and reading and spelling achievement eleven years later. *Journal of Learning Disabilities, 28*, 523–527.

Share, D., Jorm, A., Maclean, R., & Matthews, R. (1984). Sources of individual differences in reading achievement. *Journal of Educational Psychology, 76*, 1309–1324.

Stanovich, K.E. (1986). Matthew effects in reading: Some consequences of individual differences in the acquisition of literacy. *Reading Research Quarterly, 21*, 360–407.

Stanovich, K.E. (1995). Romance and reality. *The Reading Teacher, 47*, 280–291.

Stuart, M., & Coltheart, M. (1988). Does reading develop in a sequence of stages? *Cognition, 30*, 139–181.

Sulzby, E. (1983). A commentary on Ehri's critique of five studies related to letter-name knowledge and learning to read: Broadening the question. In L.M. Gentile, M.L. Kamil, & J.S. Blanchard (Eds.), *Reading research revisited*. Columbus, OH: Merrill.

Wagner, R.K., & Torgesen, J.K. (1987). The nature of phonological processing and its causal role in the acquisition of reading skills. *Psychological Bulletin, 101*, 192-212.

Yopp, H.K. (1995). A test for assessing phonemic awareness in young children. *The Reading Teacher, 49*, 20–29.

3. Isn't phonemic awareness just a 1990s word for phonics?

Ehri, L.C. (1997). Grapheme-phoneme knowledge is essential for learning to read words in English. In J.L. Metsala & L.C. Ehri (Eds.), *Word recognition in beginning literacy.* Hillsdale, NJ: Erlbaum.

Stahl, S.A., & Murray, B. (1997). Issues involved in defining phonological awareness and its relation to early reading. In J.L. Metsala & L.C. Ehri (Eds.), *Word recognition in beginning literacy.* Hillsdale, NJ: Erlbaum.

4. How does phonemic awareness work to facilitate reading acquisition?

Ehri, L.C. (1991). Development of the ability to read words. In R. Barr, M.L. Kamil, P.B. Mosenthal, & P.D. Pearson (Eds.), *Handbook of reading research: Volume 2* (pp. 383–417). White Plains, NY: Longman.

Goswami, U., & Bryant, P. (1990). *Phonological skills and learning to read.* Hove, UK: Erlbaum.

Gough, P., & Hillinger, M. (1980). Learning to read: An unnatural act. *Bulletin of the Orton Society, 30,* 180–196.

Hoover, W., & Gough, P. (1990). The simple view of reading. *Reading and Writing: An Interdisciplinary Journal, 2,* 127–160.

5. Is phonemic awareness a single, momentary insight? Or, is it best described as a skill that develops gradually over time?

Christensen, C.A. (1997). Onset, rhymes, and phonemes in learning to read. *Scientific Studies of Reading, 1,* 341–358.

Nation, K., & Hulme, C. (1997). Phonemic segmentation, not onset-rime segmentation skills, predicts early reading and spelling skills. *Reading Research Quarterly, 32,* 154–167.

Stahl, S.A., & Murray, B.A. (1994). Defining phonological awareness and its relationship to early reading. *Journal of Educational Psychology, 86,* 221–234.

Stanovich, K.E., Cunningham, A.E., & Cramer, B.B. (1984). Assessing phonological awareness in kindergarten children: Issues of task comparability. *Journal of Experimental Child Psychology, 38,* 175–190.

Yopp, H.K. (1988). The validity and reliability of phonemic awareness tests. *Reading Research Quarterly, 23,* 159–177.

6. It has been stressed that phonemic awareness is an oral language skill and that it has nothing to do with print, letters, or phonics. Is this true?

Ehri, L. (1979). Linguistic insight: Threshold of reading acquisition. In T. Waller & G.E. MacKinnon (Eds.), *Reading research: Advances in theory and practice* (Vol. 1, pp. 63–114). New York: Academic Press.

Huang, H.S., & Hanley, R.J. (1995). Phonological awareness and visual skills in learning to read Chinese and English. *Cognition, 54,* 73–98.

Huang, H.S., & Hanley, R.J. (1997). A longitudinal study of phonological skills, and Chinese reading acquisition among first-graders in Taiwan. *International Journal of Behavioral Development, 20,* 249–268.

Liberman, I., Shankweiler, D., Fischer, F., & Carter, B. (1974). Explicit syllable and phoneme segmentation in the young child. *Journal of Experimental Child Psychology, 18,* 201–212.

Mann, V. (1986). Phonological awareness: The role of reading experience. *Cognition, 24,* 65–92.

Perfetti, C., Beck, I., Bell, L., & Hughes, C. (1987). Phonemic knowledge and learning to read are reciprocal: A longitudinal study of first grade children. *Merrill-Palmer Quarterly, 33,* 283–319.

Read, C., Zhang, Y., Nie, H., & Ding, B. (1986). The ability to manipulate speech sounds depends on knowing alphabetic writing. *Cognition*, *24*, 31–45.

Wagner, R.K., Torgesen, J.K., & Rashotte, C.A. (1994). Development of reading-related phonological processing abilities: New evidence of bidirectional causality from a latent variable longitudinal study. *Developmental Psychology*, *30*, 73–87.

7. How can phonemic awareness be taught?

Baker, L., Sonnenschein, S., Serpell, R., Scher, D., Fernandez-Fein, S., Munsterman, K., Hill, S., Goddard-Truitt, V., & Danseco, E. (1996). Early literacy at home: Children's experiences and parents' perspectives. *The Reading Teacher*, *50*, 70–72.

Ball, E.W., & Blachman, B.A. (1991). Does phoneme awareness training in kindergarten make a difference in early word recognition and developmental spelling? *Reading Research Quarterly*, *26*, 49–66.

Cunningham, A.E. (1990). Explicit versus implicit instruction in phonological awareness. *Journal of Experimental Child Psychology*, *50*, 429–444.

Ehri, L.C. (1984). How orthography alters spoken language competencies in children learning to read and spell. In J. Downing & R. Valtin (Eds.), *Language awareness and learning to read* (pp. 119–147). New York: Springer-Verlag.

Lundberg, I., Frost, J., & Peterson, O.P. (1988). Effects of an extensive program for stimulating phonological awareness in preschool children. *Reading Research Quarterly*, *23*, 264–284.

McGuinness, D., McGuinness, C., & Donohue, J. (1995). Phonological training and the alphabetic principle: Evidence for reciprocal causality. *Reading Research Quarterly*, *30*, 830–853.

Scanlon, D.M., & Vellutino, F.R. (1997). A comparison of the instructional backgrounds and cognitive profiles of poor, average, and good readers who were initially identified as at risk for reading failure. *Scientific Studies of Reading*, *1*, 191–216.

Torgesen, J.K., Morgan, S.T., & Davis, C. (1992). Effects of two types of phonological awareness training on word learning in kindergarten children. *Journal of Educational Psychology*, *84*, 364–370.

Wagner, R.K., & Roshotte, C.A. (1993). *Does phonological awareness training really work? A meta-analysis.* Paper presented at the annual meeting of the American Educational Research Association, Atlanta, GA.

Winsor, P., & Pearson, P.D. (1992). *Children at risk: Their phonemic awareness development in holistic instruction* (Technical Report No. 556). Urbana, IL: Center for the Study of Reading.

8. Do all children eventually develop phonemic awareness? Shouldn't we just let them develop this understanding naturally?

Fletcher, J., Shaywitz, S., Shankweiler, D., Kayz, L., Liberman, I., Stuebing, K., Francis, D., Fowler, A., & Shaywitz, B. (1994). Cognitive profiles of reading disability: Comparisons of discrepancy and low achievement definitions. *Journal of Educational Psychology*, *86*, 6–23.

9. What does this mean for classroom practice?

Adams, M.J., & Bruck, M. (1995). Resolving the "Great Debate." *American Educator*, *8*, 7–20.

Beck, I., & Juel, C. (1995). The role of decoding in learning to read. *American Educator*, *8*, 21–25, 39–42.

Griffith, P.L., & Olson, M.W. (1992). Phonemic awareness helps beginning readers break the code. *The Reading Teacher*, *45*, 516–523.

Murray, B.A., Stahl, S.A., & Ivey, M.G. (1996). Developing phoneme awareness through alphabet books. *Reading and Writing: An Interdisciplinary Journal, 8*, 307–322.

Richgels, D., Poremba, K.J., & McGee, L.M. (1996). Kindergartners talk about print: Phonemic awareness in meaningful contexts. *The Reading Teacher, 49*, 632–642.

Yopp, H.K. (1992). Developing phonemic awareness in young children. *The Reading Teacher, 45*, 696–703.

Yopp, H.K. (1995). Read-aloud books for developing phonemic awareness: An annotated bibliography. *The Reading Teacher, 48*, 538–543.

10. What about the 20% of children who are not getting phonemic awareness by the middle of first grade?

Juel, C. (1994). *Learning to read and write in one elementary school.* New York: Springer-Verlag.

Liberman, I.Y., Shankweiler, D., & Liberman, A.M. (1991). The alphabetic principle and learning to read. In *Phonology and reading disability: Solving the reading puzzle.* Washington, DC: International Academy for Research in Learning Disabilities, U.S. Department of Health and Human Services, Public Health Service; National Institutes of Health.

Snow, C.E., Barnes, W.S., Chandler, J., Goodman, I.F., & Hemphill, L. (1991). *Unfulfilled expectations: Home and school influences on literacy.* Cambridge, MA: Harvard University Press.

Stanovich, K.E. (1986). Matthew effects in reading: Some consequences of individual differences in the acquisition of literacy. *Reading Research Quarterly, 21*, 360–407.

Torgesen, J.K., Wagner, R.K., & Rashotte, C.A. (1997). Prevention and remediation of severe reading disabilities: Keeping the end in mind. *Scientific Studies of Reading, 1*, 217–234.

Single copies of International Reading Association position statements are available in PDF format through the IRA Web site (www.reading.org/advocacy/policies). Or, send a self-addressed, stamped No. 10 envelope to International Reading Association, Attn. Dept. E.G., 800 Barksdale Road, PO Box 8139, Newark, DE 19714-8139, USA. To purchase multiple copies, visit the Association's Online Bookstore: bookstore.reading.org.

Using multiple methods of beginning reading instruction

A position statement of the International Reading Association

Historically, methods for teaching beginning reading have been the subject of controversy. The controversy is perhaps as intense as reading is important for the school children who are its focus of concern. Early reading ability influences academic success across the school curriculum, and parents, teachers, and policy makers are right to be intensely concerned. The International Reading Association has developed position statements on several important issues related to beginning reading instruction, including statements about phonics and phonemic awareness as well as a joint position statement with the National Association for the Education of Young Children, *Learning to Read and Write: Developmentally Appropriate Practices for Young Children* (1998).

The purpose of this position statement is to clarify the Association's stance on methods for teaching beginning reading (hereafter referred to as reading methods). A reading method is a set of teaching and learning materials and/or activities often given a label, such as phonics method,

literature based method, or language experience method. The essence of the position is this:

> There is no single method or single combination of methods that can successfully teach all children to read. Therefore, teachers must have a strong knowledge of multiple methods for teaching reading and a strong knowledge of the children in their care so they can create the appropriate balance of methods needed for the children they teach.

Is this position supported by research?

There is a strong research base supporting this position. Several large-scale studies of reading methods have shown that no one method is better than any other method in all settings and situations (Adams, 1990; Bond & Dykstra, 1967; Foorman et al., 1998; Hoffman, 1994; Stallings, 1975). For every method studied, some children learned to read very well while others had great difficulty. This is not a new finding. For example, in their report on the First-Grade Studies, Bond and Dykstra (1967) wrote the following:

> Children learn to read by a variety of materials and methods. Pupils become successful readers in such vastly different programs as the Language Experience approach with its relative lack of structure and vocabulary control and the various Linguistic programs with their relatively high degree of structure and vocabulary control. Furthermore, pupils experienced difficulty in each of the programs utilized. No one approach is so distinctively better in all situations and respects than the others that it should be considered the one best method and the one to be used exclusively. (p. 123)

The authors quoted Russell and Fea (1963) to illustrate their claim:

> Thinking in the field has moved away somewhat from either-or points of view about one method or set of books to a realization that different children learn in different ways, that the processes of learning to read and reading are more complex than we once thought, and that the issues in reading instruction are many sided. (p. 867)

Subsequent research has further demonstrated the naiveté of either-or viewpoints, leading Adams (1990) to conclude, "Given the tremendous variations from school to school and implementation to implementation, we should be very clear that the prescription of a method can never in itself guarantee the best of all possible outcomes" (pp. 38–39).

If there is such strong research support for this position, why is there so much controversy?

Perhaps the most important reason for this controversy is that although most children learn to read, there are a significant number of children who do not read as well as they must to function in a society that has increasing demands for literacy. The controversy results because we are not teaching reading as well as we would like to or need to.

A second reason for the controversy is that studies of reading methods are difficult to conduct and the results of such studies are difficult to interpret. Quality methods research meets many standards—such as randomly assigning children, classrooms, or schools to methods treatments; making sure that children spend the same amount of time in reading activities; and making sure that it is the method, and not just good teachers, that is responsible for the effects on the children. Random assignment to a methods treatment occurs rarely. Parents do not look kindly on arbitrary decisions about something as important as reading instruction. Controlling the time spent across classrooms is also difficult given the complexities of scheduling children in schools. And determining whether it is the teacher or the methods that are having an effect means that the same teacher—or teachers who are somehow "equivalent"—must teach the competing methods. (For an extended treatment of this topic see Pressley & Allington, in press.)

Because of the difficulty of conducting good reading methods research, results are sometimes confusing. For most methods some studies find statistically significant differences, some do not find differences, and there are some for which the findings are not conclusive one way or the other. Another reason for the inconclusive results is that some methods may work for some children and not for others.

One of the major difficulties in methods research is defining the term *reading method*, a term that has led to more confusion than clarity. Reading method is a broad label that describes actual classroom teaching in a very general way. Many different activities are used to teach young children to read. In addition, specific arrangements and materials within the classroom environment support children's literacy learning. There are many different ways these activities, arrangements, and materials may be incorporated in a classroom. Not surprisingly, many reading methods combine teaching activities from a number of different sources to develop a coherent program for teaching beginning reading. A given reading method may emphasize a particular aspect of teaching beginning reading and so be said to use a "phonics" method, a "whole language" method, a "code-emphasis" method, a "literature-based" method, or a "meaning-emphasis" method. However, some of the *same* activities may occur in classrooms that use *different* "methods." For example, teachers in both code-emphasis and meaning-emphasis programs may use phonics lessons, read books aloud to children, and have children take books home to read. Often reading methods studies do not give clear descriptions of what is actually occurring in the classroom; hence the particular "method" is not well defined.

Another problem with methods studies is that our measures of what "works" are not defined consistently. What do we mean when we say a method works? In some studies a method works if children are able to read lists of words in isolation. In others "works" means that children can answer questions on a multiple-choice test. If there is anything we have learned from methods studies, it is that children learn what we teach them (Pearson & Fielding, 1991). If we teach them how to pronounce pseudowords, they learn how to pronounce pseudowords and sometimes lists of regular words. If we teach children to summarize, they learn how to give better summaries. Therefore, many methods have a right to claim they "work," but that does not necessarily mean that any of these methods are better than all or most other methods or that any one of them is the "right" method. For all these reasons beginning reading instruction has been controversial.

Given the difficulty of conducting and interpreting methods studies, what do we know about teaching beginning reading?

Although there is controversy about how to teach children to read, there is less controversy about what it is that children need to learn. A great deal of research evidence converges on the following definition of reading (see also Snow, Burns, & Griffin, 1998):

Reading is a complex system of deriving meaning from print that requires all of the following:

- the development and maintenance of a motivation to read
- the development of appropriate active strategies to construct meaning from print
- sufficient background information and vocabulary to foster reading comprehension
- the ability to read fluently
- the ability to decode unfamiliar words
- the skills and knowledge to understand how phonemes or speech sounds are connected to print

A skilled beginning reading teacher is a professional who knows what this definition means, can assess children in light of the definition, and then can adjust the balance of methods so that each child is taught what he or she needs to learn.

What methods are available for teaching beginning reading?

We know that a sound and effective beginning reading program must incorporate a variety of activities in order to give children positive attitudes toward literacy, as well as the knowledge, strategies, and skills they need to be successful readers. Studies point to a number of instructional practices that can promote young children's literacy learning. All of these practices can be effective, depending on how well they fit with children's needs in learning to read. For example, children who already know letter-sound correspondences are not likely to benefit from training in phonemic awareness (International Reading Association, 1998). Children who can use predictable language to read a book are not likely to benefit from having the teacher read the whole book to them in advance, as in shared reading (Johnston, 1997/1998). The questions of how these activities should be combined and how much time should be devoted to each are best answered through studies in the particular settings of concern. For more information about best practices refer to *Learning to Read and Write: Developmentally Appropriate Practices for Young Children* (International Reading Association & National Association for the Education of Young Children, 1998) and *Preventing Reading Difficulties in Young Children* (Snow, Burns, & Griffin, 1998).

Who should decide the content of beginning reading instruction?

Because there is no clearly documented best way to teach beginning reading, professionals who are closest to the children must be the ones to make the decisions about what reading methods to use, and they must have the flexibility to modify those methods when they determine that particular children are not learning. These are the facts behind the International Reading Association's (1998) resolution on policy mandates for reading methods, which includes the following statements:

> If we are to be successful in promoting reading achievement, we must locate decision making at the point of service to students. Broad mandates can intrude on or even replace professional decision making, resulting in instruction that is least responsive to student needs. Ultimately the effects of such mandates are to reduce the quality of instruction in schools and classrooms and to limit the potential for all students to be successful in learning to read.

What are the implications of this position at the federal, state, district, and school levels?

Legislation at the federal and state levels should not prescribe particular methods. At the federal level policy makers should provide resources, particularly for schools and children in high poverty settings, that allow school districts to provide professional development in reading instruction, and that enable them to provide appropriate reading material. Policy makers also must support further research on successful practice, deriving from a range of perspectives. Policy makers also should support decision-making processes at the state, district, and school level.

Policy makers also should support balanced approaches to reading instruction at the state level. Policy makers should provide funds for professional development. State standards and language arts frameworks should promote a balanced view of reading instruction that attends to all the features of the definition of reading offered here. Policy makers also should provide funding for the purchase of books that children can read on their own and enjoy.

School districts must develop reading programs that meet the needs of all children. School districts should provide guidelines that ensure that all children are allotted adequate time for reading. School districts also should provide the necessary professional development activities so that teachers can provide a balanced approach to reading instruction. School districts must enlist the support of parents in developing teachers' knowledge of their children and involve them in the academic progress of their children. School districts must show, using multiple measures, that federal, state, and local resources have been used to improve children's reading.

We end this position statement with a call issued by Bond and Dykstra (1967) in their report on the First-Grade Studies.

> Future research might well center on teacher and learning situation characteristics rather than method and materials. The tremendous range among classrooms within any method points out the importance of elements in the learning situation over and above the methods employed. To improve reading instruction, it is necessary to train better teachers of reading rather than to expect a panacea in the form of materials. (p. 123)

References

Adams, M.J. (1990). *Beginning to read: Thinking and learning about print*. Cambridge,

MA: Massachusetts Institute of Technology Press.

Bond, G.L., & Dykstra, R. (1967). The cooperative research program in first-grade reading instruction. *Reading Research Quarterly, 2,* 10–141.

Foorman, B.R., Francis, D.J., Fletcher, J.M., Schatschneider, C., & Mehta, P. (1998). The role of instruction in learning to read: Preventing reading failure in at-risk children. *Journal of Educational Psychology, 90,* 37–55.

Hoffman, J.V. (1994). So what's new in the new basals? A focus in first grade. *Journal of Reading Behavior, 26,* 47–73.

International Reading Association. (1998, May). *Resolution on policy mandates.* Adopted by the delegates assembly at the 43rd Annual Convention of the International Reading Association, Orlando, FL.

International Reading Association & National Association for the Education of Young Children. (1998). *Learning to read and write: Developmentally appropriate practices for young children.* Newark, DE: International Reading Association; Washington, DC: National Association for the Education of Young Children.

Johnston, P. (1997/1998). Commentary on a critique. *The Reading Teacher, 51,* 282–285.

Pearson, P.D., & Fielding, L. (1991). Comprehension instruction. In R. Barr, M.L. Kamil, P. Mosenthal, & P.D. Pearson (Eds.), *Handbook of reading research: Volume II* (pp. 815–860). White Plains, NY: Longman.

Pressley, M., & Allington, R. (in press). What should reading research be the research of? *Issues in Education.*

Russell, D.H., & Fea, H. (1963). Research on teaching reading. In N.L. Gage (Ed.), *Handbook of Research in Teaching* (pp. 865–928). Chicago: Rand McNally.

Snow, C.E., Burns, M.S., & Griffin, P. (Eds.). (1998). *Preventing reading difficulties in young children.* Washington, DC: National Academy Press.

Stallings, J. (1975). Implementation and child effects of teaching practices in follow through classrooms. *Monographs of the Society for Research in Child Development, 40,* 7–8.

Single copies of International Reading Association position statements are available in PDF format through the IRA Web site (www.reading.org/advocacy/policies). Or, send a self-addressed, stamped No. 10 envelope to International Reading Association, Attn. Dept. E.G., 800 Barksdale Road, PO Box 8139, Newark, DE 19714-8139, USA. To purchase multiple copies, visit the Association's Online Bookstore: bookstore.reading.org.